Lemon Law

The Standard Reference Guide

Norman F. Taylor: Attorney at Law

Wallace Publishing

Glendale, California

Published by
Wallace Publishing
425 W. Broadway
Suite 220
Glendale, CA 91204

Design, Layout & Illustrations
Peter Green Design
127 S. Brand Blvd.
Suite 330
Glendale, California 91204

International Standard Book Number (ISBN) 0-9760058-0-8
Library of Congress Control Number: 2004115124

This book has been printed and designed using the
Adobe Software program InDesign CS®.

Printed in South Korea
First Printing

Disclaimer

This publication is intended to give an overview of the information presented, and should
never be used as a substitute for seeking expert advice. I have done my best to give you useful
and accurate information. Please be aware, however, that laws and procedures are constantly
changing and are subject to differing interpretations. This publication cannot substitute for the
independent judgment and skills of a competent attorney or other professional. Non-attorneys
are cautioned against using these materials to conduct a lawsuit without advice or assistance
from an attorney. Non-attorneys are also cautioned against engaging in conduct that might be
considered the unauthorized practice of law.

This book is dedicated to my best friend, Preston Kennedy Taylor.

Acknowledgments

I want to thank every consumer who has drawn a line in the sand, who has said, *"I am not going to live with a defective car, boat, or motor home, and I am going to do something about it. I will not give up and go away."*

Special thanks go to

Donald Ladew for his friendship and support throughout this project, without whose contributions this book would not have been possible.

Bret Shefter, Esq., who has been with me for eleven years. His loyalty and supreme legal acumen not only contributed to this book but have allowed me to build a law practice that is well respected in the legal community.

Rene Korper, Esq., who has been with me for eight years as our principal litigator. Without his insatiable appetite to do battle with manufacturers, I would not have had the luxury of time to write this book.

Rosemary Shahan, who, through her fine work at Consumers for Auto Reliability and Safety (CARS), has made our world a safer place to live.

Rosemary Delderfield, whose superlative proofreading made this book much better than the author imagined. Thank you.

My staff who are the best support group imaginable.

Table of Contents

PREFACE   XI

INTRODUCTION   XIII

HOW TO USE THIS BOOK   XV

PART 1   The Lemon Stories

Chapter 1   *A New Car Lemon Story*   3

             Introduction   3

             Visits to the Dealer   5

             A Summary of New Car Misery   13

Chapter 2   *A Motor Home Lemon Story*   15

             An American Dream   15

             The Pitfalls of Multiple Warranties   20

             A Summary of Motor Home Misery   23

Chapter 3   *A Used Car Lemon Story*   25

             Ms. Peters Bought a Used Car   25

             A Summary of the Used Car Story   31

PART 2   Why We Need Lemon Laws

Chapter 4   *A Brief History of Lemon Law*   35

             In the Beginning There Was Commercial Chaos 35

Chapter 5   *The Need for Lemon Law*   43

             Introduction to the Need for Lemon Law   43

             Quantity vs. Quality   44

             The Chain of Modern Economics   47

             Volume of Defective Consumer Goods   51

             Complexity and Malfunctions: A Catch-22   52

             How Many People Just Give Up?   59

Chapter 6	*Manufacturer-Dealership Relationship*	61
	It's a Business Relationship	61
	Secret Warranties	63
	The Flat-Rate Pay System for Technicians	68
	When the Dealership Is in Trouble	75
Chapter 7	*The Gauntlet*	79
	"If You Can't Fix Their Car, Fix Their Head"	79
	The Gauntlet: What Did I Do to Deserve This?	80
	Entering the Gauntlet	82
	Stupid Dealer Tricks	84
	Stupid Manufacturer Tricks	91
	Informal Dispute Resolution: Arbitration	95
PART 3	**The Lemon Law and You**	
Chapter 8	*How Can I Tell If My Vehicle Is a Lemon?*	99
	What Is a Lemon?	99
	What Is a Defect?	101
	What Is Substantial Impairment?	102
	Impaired Value	104
	Reasonable Opportunity to Repair	106
	The Lemon Law Presumption	110
Chapter 9	*Warranty and the Broken Promise*	117
	Warranty Overview	117
	Express Warranties	118
	Implied Warranties	120
	Service Contracts	123
	Service Contract Questions and Answers	129
	"As Is" Sale	130

Chapter 10	*Replacement or Refund: Choosing a Remedy*	133
	Definition of Remedy	133
	Refund	134
	Replacement	136
	Incidental and Consequential Damages	138
Chapter 11	*Manufacturer Defenses*	143
	Introduction to Defenses	143
	Driver Abuse	144
	Vehicle Neglect	147
	Statute of Limitations	148
Chapter 12	*Litigation*	151
	Introduction to Litigation	151
	To Arbitrate or Not to Arbitrate	151
	Before Litigation	154
	Selecting an Attorney	155
	Attorneys' Fees: Can I Afford to Sue?	160
	Litigation	162
	Civil Penalty	165
Chapter 13	*Lemon Laundering*	167
	What Is Laundering?	167
	Buybacks Are Different	169
	A Lemon Is a Lemon Is a Lemon	170
	What Can You Do About It?	173
Appendix A	*Lemon Law Summary All Fifty States*	177
Appendix B	*Bibliography*	233
Appendix C	*Glossary*	237
Index		243

Preface

To every dealership across the United States doing its best to get it right, doing its best to provide high-quality services and repairs at a fair price: we know you are out there. We do not, by any means, lump you together with those who systematically abuse the trust of consumers and knowingly destroy their belief in a fair deal.

Owning a new automobile or motor home is an American dream. It ranks right up there with owning a home. When such dreams are laid waste, people descend into cynicism and discontent. All hardworking American citizens deserve the opportunity to take pride in the fruits of their labors. When you purchase a new car or motor home, you should be able to point to your vehicle with satisfaction and look forward to many years of pleasure in the accomplishment. Your buying experience should never include frustration, helplessness, betrayal, months or even years lost, or your hard-earned money down the drain. Unfortunately, this is an all-too-common American nightmare.

We are a country of laws. Yes, it would be better if these laws weren't necessary, but the reality is that corporate greed and indifference exist. We can be thankful that we do have laws, and the means to enforce them when necessary. This is a very good thing, if for no other reason than to remind those who would abuse our trust to take heed, for they will certainly be brought to justice. They will be held accountable for their actions.

If ever you find yourself in any of the situations described in this book, do not give in. Do not "go away." To do so is to encourage those who betray your trust to move on to even greater and more despicable behavior. It may be difficult to keep in mind those who will follow you into the manufacturer/dealership gauntlet, but your demand for fairness, and proper application of the law, will affect their travel down that same path.

The law is made strong and effective by its continued application. Just as a child needs to be constantly reminded of the limits of bad behavior, so do those in the business world. Be part of the chain of personal and corporate responsibility. Say to them, *"No! I am not giving in; I am not going to go away."*

NORMAN F. TAYLOR

Introduction

The Latin phrase *caveat emptor*, or *let the buyer beware*, has accompanied the buying and selling of goods since at least the 1600s, and probably much earlier. Essentially, it means that if you buy something, you are on your own as to whether you got what you paid for. The concept has probably been around since the first Neanderthal traded an axe head to his neighbor, although what passed for warranty law in those ancient times was probably a bit more direct. If the axe Ooog the Neanderthal traded to his neighbor Moog was **substantially impaired** in **use**, **value**, or **safety**, Moog probably visited the side of Ooog's head with a large rock. We are slightly more civilized now.

Early warranty enforcement technique.

The stories of those who have purchased defective goods would fill a hundred books. Almost everyone has had a bad experience buying something that didn't live up to the promotional hype.

If you buy a bad hair dryer, you might say, *"Well, that's the last time I buy anything made by those people."* But what happens when it's the largest purchase you have ever made outside of a house, and you are obligated to make large monthly payments for the next five years? It's not that easy to let it go, to just ignore it.

Today, the average vehicle owner hasn't a chance of repairing his own car.

This is especially true if the purchase is an automobile or a motor home. Vehicles are complicated machines, and are becoming more so as computer technology advances. Today's consumer has the benefit of better running, more efficient, and more reliable vehicles. However, these machines are so complex that when something goes wrong the average consumer hasn't a chance of repairing it. They are generally at the mercy of the local dealership to determine the cause and repair the problem.

It's no fun being on the receiving end when manufacturers and their dealerships won't take responsibility for defects in the cars they sell, even though they know the defects exist. This book is an attempt to put you in the driver's seat.

Your time, money, and peace of mind should be yours to control. We are going to help you take charge of this part of your life.

Let this Latin phrase be your battle cry:

> Caveat venditor: Let the seller beware!

How to Use This Book

I have attempted to make this book as real as seventeen years of experience in every kind of warranty law can make it. The situations and events described herein have happened to people just like you.

Who Should Use This Book

I have tried to design this book to be useful to several different kinds of readers. They include

- consumers who want to know if they have a lemon vehicle now;

- consumers who want to avoid the pitfalls of owning a lemon vehicle by becoming knowledgeable on the subject;

- members of the legal community, all levels;

- manufacturers and dealers interested in taking back lost ground from foreign markets through honesty and quality in manufacturing and in service.

Layout of the Book

We have tried not
to limit this book to
California lemon
law only.

This book is constructed in sections addressing specific areas of current warranty law. All fifty states have some kind of *lemon law*. I address California lemon law specifically because I practice law in this state, and because California lemon law has served as a model for many other states. Not everything in this book will be important to you. While each person's situation is unique, there are many points common to all cases.

Read the Lemon Stories first. The Lemon Stories are where the meat is. I recommend that you then leaf through the Table of Contents and find the areas of interest that best describe your situation.

If you are outside of California, most concepts found here are applicable with the exception of those peculiar to your state's lemon law.

> I have tried to include the things that will help you take on the big corporations and win. Knowledge truly is power.

The Lemon Stories

If Mr. and Mrs. Jones went to the Sleazy Cars R Us used car lot to purchase a car "as is," any misery that followed would be their problem. But when they go to General Motors, Chrysler, Mercedes-Benz, Ford, or any of the automobile giants, Mr. and Mrs. Jones have a right to expect more.

The first three chapters present three lemon stories covering a large portion of typical lemon law issues. Many of the problems described in the Lemon Stories may sound familiar to you.

- **Story I**: A typical example of a new car purchase

- **Story II**: A typical example of a motor home purchase

- **Story III**: A typical example of a used car purchase, with the remainder of the manufacturer's new car warranty and the dealership's used car warranty

The key elements of these stories are

- the mileage on the vehicle

- the number of repair attempts

- whether the defects substantially impair the vehicle's use, value, or safety to the owner.

My purpose is to show in the simplest terms, and in a natural way, situations that may be familiar to you. Every fact, every point of law, from beginning to end, is real.

The sequence of actions in these stories follows actual events as they have happened to real people purchasing new or used vehicles in the United States today. Chapters 1, 2, and 3 are real examples, but I think they are your stories as well.

Important Note

> I want to stress again the importance of reading the Lemon Stories of chapters 1, 2, and 3 before going on to those chapters containing more detailed material.

Simple Language vs. Legalese

The law, like engineering, medicine, and so many other professions, has its own technical language. Most of you don't have time to learn this language, and I am not going to burden you with it. If legal points of law are needed to support a particular issue, footnotes will direct you to more detailed information.

The body of warranty law is large. Those of you who are not part of the legal profession will find what you need to know to make good decisions if you think you have a lemon vehicle or if you want to avoid having one.

Following Time, Mileage, Days in the Shop

In warranty law, **when** things happen is important. I have included the dates for each part of each story. In the stories, we also keep track of the number of days the vehicle is in the shop.

Warranty and mileage are also tied together in ways that are poorly understood. In subsequent chapters I will talk about how this may affect you.

Footnotes and References

As you are reading through the stories of consumers and their "lemon wars," you will see footnotes referencing other chapters. These chapters cover various parts of warranty law more thoroughly.

If you want to know more about a particular point of warranty law, go directly to the referenced chapter and read the material.

State-by-State Lemon Law Summary

At the back of the book is a thorough summary of every state's lemon law. While there are certain functional aspects that are always present in these statutes, there is considerable variation from state to state.

PART 1

The Lemon Stories

CHAPTER 1

A New Car Lemon Story

> *"Caveat emptor: Let the buyer beware."*
> —Latin Proverb

Introduction

Jim and Sandy Jones were a typical family of four. They had two children, a ten-year-old son and a seven-year-old daughter. As is so common in these times, they both worked: Mr. Jones was a plumber and Mrs. Jones sold real estate. Mrs. Jones was the primary driver of the family car. Besides using the vehicle to take clients to view houses, she was also *Mom's Taxi Service:* she chauffeured the children to school, ballet lessons, Little League Baseball, and many other activities.

Mr. and Mrs. Jones Go Shopping

Mr. and Mrs. Jones decided it was time to replace the family car. They decided to buy a new car, rather than a used car, so that they could enjoy the wonderful feeling of trouble-free transportation. After visits to several dealers, they settled on the car of their choice, a Sport Utility Vehicle (SUV),[1] and negotiated the purchase price. This was their first new vehicle; it should have been an exciting event. They picked up their brand-new vehicle the next day.

---

1. See appendix C for a definition of *SUV.*

New Car Purchase Contract

Here are the details of Mr. and Mrs. Jones's purchase:

- The purchase price was $32,000.

- The manufacturer gave a three-year/36,000-mile bumper-to-bumper written warranty.

- Financing: Amount down = $5,000; Number of years on loan = 5; Interest rate = 6.75%; Monthly payment = $300.

As is often the case in the real world, unforeseen things happen. The dealership could not install the alarm system when Mr. and Mrs. Jones bought their vehicle because it didn't have enough units in stock. The dealer gave them a Due Bill for this incomplete action.[2]

The Jones's Drive Home in Their New Car

Date: 7/16
Mileage = 5

Your first new car! Living the American dream.

When Mr. and Mrs. Jones drove away from the dealership in their new car, they were excited and proud. It was the American dream.

As they approached the first red light, the vehicle's Check Engine light came on and their brand-new SUV stalled. Imagine the disbelief, the bewilderment, the stress, and the blaring horns of those behind them!

After the engine had been cranked far too long, it finally started. They drove home, not quite as happy, not quite as proud.[3]

They called the dealership the next day. The service department said it could schedule an appointment in two weeks. It was too busy to take the car.[4]

---

2. See appendix C for a definition of *Due Bill*.
3. See chapter 8, 108, The *Shaken Faith* Doctrine.
4. See chapter 7, 84, We Can't Take Your Car Now.

During the two weeks while Mr. and Mrs. Jones waited, they put 1,500 miles on the car. They were busy people. Also during this period, the Check Engine light came on several times and the car stalled each time. Once when Mrs. Jones was about to make a left turn in front of traffic, with her children in the car, the Check Engine light came on and again the car stalled. An accident was barely averted. It was a very dangerous situation.

They also discovered that the air conditioning generated an odor better left in a locker room.[5] This was a real problem, as their son, Timmy, had asthma and it acted up every time he was in the car.

Recent research indicates that air-conditioner-induced mold problems are much more widespread than previously imagined.

Visits to the Dealer

First Visit: Bewildered

After two weeks of waiting impatiently, Mrs. Jones took the car to the dealer. There she met a person called a service writer.[6] She described as well as possible what she and her husband experienced driving the car. She also told the service writer about the air conditioning. He wrote up the repair order.

Date: 7/30
Mileage = 1,510

1st repair order written.

Keep in mind that Mrs. Jones wasn't an auto mechanic, so her description wasn't technical. She described the sounds she heard and what the car did. She also expressed her emotional response: remember, she almost had an accident as a result of the defect.

Sometimes there is a striking difference between what the owner describes as a problem and what the service writer puts on the repair order. A service writer may try to write a repair order in a way that makes sense to the mechanic. Other times, however, the service writer may alter the customer's comments to make the problem look like something it is not.[7]

It is important to know exactly at what point in time and at what mileage the defect is first presented to the dealer for repair.

5. See http://www.mold-kill.com/isozonesafe.html.
6. See appendix C for a definition of *service writer*.
7. See chapter 7, 85, "Slicing and Dicing" the Defect.

Always pay close attention to what the service writer puts on the repair order.

Didn't return calls: a common dealer delay.

Date: 8/04
Days in Shop = 6
Total Days in Shop = 6

In this case the service writer told Mrs. Jones that the problem could be in the Emission Control System (ECS), and that is what he wrote on the repair order.

Mrs. Jones called repeatedly for several days.[8] Finally the dealership's personnel told her that she could come and pick up her car. When she asked what the problem was, they told her that they had fixed a vacuum hose. She asked about the air conditioning smell and they told her they had sprayed a special chemical in the air conditioning vent to suppress the odor. She picked up the car and drove home. The excitement and pride of ownership were temporarily restored.

Second Visit: Frustrated

Five weeks and 2,000 miles later, the problem occurred again: the Check Engine light came on and the car stalled. Now she was afraid to take the car anywhere, knowing she might be stranded. Mrs. Jones called the service center again and asked for an appointment. She was told they were too busy and could not fit her in for another ten days. During those ten days, she added another 1,000 nervous miles to the car, and when she drove her kids, she traded cars with her husband so that they wouldn't have to risk riding in the defective SUV.

Date: 9/15
Mileage = 4,505

When Mrs. Jones finally got to the dealership, she described the problem to the service writer. She reminded him that this was the second time she had brought the car in for the same thing. She also reported that the air conditioning still smelled awful.

Mrs. Jones told them about her son's asthma, and that he had several times had attacks in the car.

---

8. See chapter 8, 107, Days Out of Service.

The service writer wrote the repair order, but Mrs. Jones noted that he wasn't writing down exactly what she said. She asked him about this and he said, *"Oh, we don't have to write everything down; we only need to get the general idea."* She left her vehicle and again had to find a ride home.

2nd repair order written.

After six days, the service center called and said, *"Mrs. Jones, the mechanic found and replaced a defective emission control valve."* She asked about the air conditioning again, and they said, *"We fixed that, Mrs. Jones."*

Date: 9/20
Mileage = 4,505
Days in Shop = 6
Total Days in Shop = 12

"That darn air conditioner! Pull over, Jim;
Timmy's having another allergy attack!"

Third Visit: Openly Hostile

Two months and 4,000 miles later, it happened again! Mrs. Jones was driving the children to school. The Check Engine light came on and the car stalled. By now, Mrs. Jones thought of the car as *"that piece of crap we stupidly wasted our money on,"* or had even less charitable thoughts.

Date: 11/20
Mileage = 8,505

After endless cranking, she finally got it started, dropped her children off at school, and drove straight to the dealership. There, she got a familiar story. *"We're too busy. We have a slot for you in a week or so."* This time Mrs. Jones insisted—all right, she may have shouted—*"You have to take it now! You have to fix it today!"* Considering her history with the vehicle, it is understandable that she got a little emotional.

3rd repair order written.

At this point nothing had been fixed.

The dealership agreed to take the car. The repair order was written. Mrs. Jones reported the faulty air conditioning again, and that it was still producing a musty odor like dirty socks.

When she was leaving, Mrs. Jones asked about a loaner. She had to have a car to get around, and she couldn't keep imposing on her friends. The service writer told her, *"Sorry, we don't have a loaner car for you. We've given out all our free cars."* Mrs. Jones replied, *"I don't care; I'll rent one. You just fix the darn car!"* She got a rental car.[9]

Date: 11/28
Mileage = 8,520
Days in Shop = 9
Total Days in Shop = 21

Eight days later the service writer called and said the mechanic had found a plugged canister purge valve and replaced it. When she asked about the air conditioning, he said that they had "ozonated" it.[10] She picked up the car and drove home.

Fourth Visit: Fear and Loathing at the Dealership

Six weeks and 3,500 miles later, Mrs. Jones was driving on the freeway, taking her daughter to a ballet recital. The Check Engine light came on and the car stalled in the fast lane. It was pretty scary. She called her husband and the Auto Club, and waited to be towed. She and her daughter missed the recital.

9. See chapter 10, 138, Incidental and Consequential Damages.
10. See appendix C for a definition of *ozonation*.

Stalled on the freeway: white knuckles,
white hair, and possibly much worse!

The car was towed to the dealership. The next day, Mr. Jones decided to call the manufacturer's toll-free number. He described the problems to a customer service agent.[11] She seemed very sympathetic and suggested that Mr. Jones take the car to a different dealership.

Mr. Jones called the service writer at the selling dealership and told him what the manufacturer's customer service agent suggested. The service writer said, *"Fine. We couldn't find anything wrong anyway."*[12] Mrs. Jones picked up the vehicle, but the dealership did not give her a repair order. When she asked about it, the service writer told her, *"We didn't do anything."*[13]

Customer service people "seem" so helpful, but nothing happens.

Date: 1/14
Mileage = 12,020
Days in Shop = 2
Total Days in Shop = 23

Bells and whistles should go off if, for any reason, the dealer doesn't write a repair order.

11. See chapter 7, 91, The *Glad Hand.*
12. See chapter 7, 87, No Problem Found.
13. See chapter 7, 90, No Repair Order Is Written.

Fifth Visit: More Runaround with a Lie

This is not true in most states.

The next day, Mrs. Jones took the car to the recommended dealership. She told the service writer the whole unpleasant history, including what the manufacturer's customer service agent had suggested. The service writer said, *"I understand, but we can't work on your car. You have to have it worked on by the people who sold it to you."*

No repair order written at second dealership.

No matter what Mrs. Jones said, the service writer insisted that she take the car back to the selling dealership.[14] The second dealership didn't write a repair order, even though Mrs. Jones had presented the vehicle for repair.[15] Mrs. Jones brought the car home and told her husband what happened.

Sixth Visit: Enter the Specialist

Date: 1/26
Mileage = 12,220
Days in Shop = 10
Total Days in Shop = 33

Mr. Jones called the manufacturer's Consumer Hotline again. He told the manufacturer's customer service agent that they better stop messing around with his wife, telling her to go here, go there; he was darn well tired of it. The agent said, *"I understand. What I want you to do is take the car to a different dealership. We have a field technical specialist there who will investigate the problem."*[16]

Bring on the engineers, the specialists: more flimflam.

Once again, no repair order was written at the third dealership.

Mrs. Jones called the third dealership and was given an appointment two weeks later. When she dropped off the car, she wasn't given an opportunity to describe the problems to the field technical specialist—in fact, she never even saw the specialist. Again, no repair order was written.

14. See chapter 8, 109, More on Accurate Repair Orders.
15. See chapter 7, 90, No Repair Order Is Written.
16. See chapter 7, 92, Try a Different Technician.

"We checked the semi-craniflanset and the dynamic flatulence interchange modulator on our new billion-dollar diagnostic device. No problem was found, Mrs. Jones."

Ten days later the representative at the third dealership called Mrs. Jones and reported that the specialist, after exhaustive tests, found nothing wrong with the vehicle.

No More Visits: They Try Arbitration

At work, Mr. Jones related the story of his car difficulties to a co-worker. The co-worker said, *"My attorney might be able to help you. Here's his number. Give him a call."*

Instead, they decided to call the Consumer Hotline one more time. This time Mr. Jones asked, *"What's this about the lemon law? Do we have rights? Do we qualify?"* The manufacturer's agent replied, *"No, you have to go through arbitration first"*[17]

In California and some other states this is another lie.

17. See chapter 12, 151, To Arbitrate or Not to Arbitrate.

Mr. and Mrs. Jones filled out the necessary forms. They imagined that they might get a fair hearing about what was really wrong with their car. Perhaps someone would finally help, someone would really listen!

After a month-long wait, and another 2,000 miles on the car, the arbitration was held. The arbitrator noted that no problem had been found on two separate occasions, and that at least once it had been determined that Mrs. Jones had failed to replace the gas cap properly. The arbitrator concluded that Mr. and Mrs. Jones had not proven that the manufacturer had not successfully repaired the Check Engine light defect.

The arbitrator also found that, even if something were still wrong with the vehicle, the manufacturer did not have a reasonable opportunity to repair it, because the dealerships had performed repairs only three times.

Mr. and Mrs. Jones told the arbitrator that the air conditioning had never been repaired during any of the visits to the dealerships. The manufacturer never said anything about this defect because its field technical specialist had not even looked at it. However, the arbitrator found that the defective air conditioning might not be considered to **substantially impair the use, value, or safety** of the vehicle. Still, the arbitrator ordered the dealership to repair the air conditioning again.

Ordering the manufacturer to fix the air conditioning made it appear as though Mr. and Mrs. Jones won something. They didn't win anything. The manufacturer's warranty still covered the defective air conditioner, so the manufacturer was already obligated to attempt to repair it again.[18]

> Why would the arbitrator assume that she didn't know how to put a gas cap on properly? Was it because Mrs. Jones is a woman?

> It is really quite absurd to tell someone they can have what they are already entitled to.

---

18. See chapter 7, 92, We Want to Reward You for Your Patience.

At this point, many car owners would have been in apathy about the whole situation. They would have given up, and perhaps traded in their defective vehicle for a new car.[19] Mr. and Mrs. Jones did not give up. They did not go away. They retained a lemon law attorney.

When you give up and go away, you provide the manufacturer with the incentive to continue their policy of deception and delay.

A Summary of New Car Misery

- The vehicle was defective from the moment the Joneses picked it up.

- They offered the vehicle repeatedly to the dealerships for repair.

- They got only three repair orders; they should have had six.

- There was a serious safety defect that never got repaired.

- The vehicle was in the shop for more than thirty days.

- They were given false and misleading information.

19. See chapter 7, 90, Dealer Offers to Sell You a New Car.

CHAPTER 2
A Motor Home Lemon Story

> *"If ever the pleasure of one has to be bought with the pain of the other, there better be no trade. A trade by which one gains and the other loses is a fraud."*
> —Dagny Taggart
> *Atlas Shrugged*, Ayn Rand

An American Dream

Another great American dream: retire, buy a motor home, and see the country. Eduardo and Luisa Rodriguez worked hard all their lives. The children were living their own lives, and it was time for Mr. and Mrs. Rodriguez to enjoy theirs. They planned to sell their home and use part of the proceeds to purchase a motor home.

They decided on a mid-range RV that was within their budget yet large enough for comfort. They also decided on a new vehicle, as they didn't want to live with other people's mistakes.

They Took Delivery in a Different State

Mr. and Mrs. Rodriguez lived in Nevada. They were in California on vacation and happened to drive by an RV dealership. They stopped in, saw the model they liked, and started discussing the purchase. The motor home cost $150,000, but the salesperson told them that they would also have to pay California sales tax, which was thousands of dollars more.

Mr. and Mrs. Rodriguez decided to wait until they got back to Nevada to buy a new motor home. The salesperson said he knew of a way they could buy the motor home from his dealership without paying California sales tax. On the advice of the dealership, Mr. and Mrs. Rodriguez agreed to take delivery in Nevada, where there is no state sales tax.

This is not illegal. It does, however, raise jurisdictional issues: the question of which state's laws apply. You should consult with an attorney before taking delivery away from the dealer's facilities.

Multiple Warranties

Because several companies manufactured different major components of the motor home, Mr. and Mrs. Rodriguez received more than one warranty:

- **Chassis**, two years or 24,000 miles

- **Engine and transmission**, five years or 50,000 miles

- **Motor home living area**, two years regardless of mileage

- Other miscellaneous warranties for such things as appliances

"Just read these when you get home, Mr. Rodriguez."

First Visit: The Defects

Mr. and Mrs. Rodriguez received their motor home in Nevada and drove off to see America. Four weeks and 5,000 miles later, water leaks and other problems forced them to stop in Van Horn, Texas.

Date: 5/30
Mileage = 5,000

- There was a serious leak in the roof. Water was seeping into the vehicle, ruining walls, wood, and carpet.

- There was a dangerous handling problem. When driving they noticed that turning was difficult. It was as if the front wheels weren't making proper contact with the road.[1]

1. This Internet article covers RV weight and balance issues. Go to http://www.campingworld.com/tLibrary/output.cfm?ID=185311.

"This vehicle was designed for that soft,
cushiony feel, Mr. Rodriguez. Pretty cool, huh?"

This weight
problem is known
among RVers as
the infamous "tail
wagging the dog"
phenomenon.

Much later, Mr. and Mrs. Rodriguez learned the cause of this problem. The weight of the RV was poorly distributed toward the rear of the vehicle, causing the front end to rise. This caused the front tires to have poor contact with the ground, which made steering difficult and handling hazardous.

Their vehicle had what is called a *slide-out,* a room in the motor home that extends outward on rails to create more space inside the coach. The slide-out had several associated defects:

- Sometimes when they turned a corner, the slide-out extended on its own. This was very frightening, and certainly a safety issue.

- The bad fit of the slide-out allowed sand and dust to enter the motor home.

- The slide-out tore the interior carpet near the sides.

- Because there were bad seals around the slide-out, there were air leaks and an unpleasant whistling noise whenever they were on the highway.

This is a typical list. We've certainly seen worse.

The RV had a number of other problems:

- The shower doors stuck and couldn't be opened.

- The rearview mirrors were damaged.

- There were numerous trim defects (paint, molding, drawer handles, etc.).

First Repair Attempt

Mr. and Mrs. Rodriguez called the coach manufacturer, who gave them the names of the nearest authorized repair facilities. However, unlike automobiles, motor homes don't have dealerships and repair facilities in every city and town. There were no repair facilities close to Van Horn, Texas, so they had a choice: an independent shop in Abilene, or a dealership in Dallas.

Date: 5/30
Mileage = 5,330

Date: 5/30
Mileage = 5,330
Days in shop = 3
Total Days in Shop = 3

This is a house on wheels. Successful repairs need a wide spectrum of skills that may go beyond that of most ordinary mechanics.

Motor home repair facilities can't stock every part needed. They must be sent for, and this takes time, often a long time.

Date: 6/30
Mileage = 5,510
Days in Shop = 27
Total Days in Shop = 30

They drove to the closer facility in Abilene. They gave the mechanic their extensive list of problems, and he put them on a repair order. Two days later, the mechanic told them their motor home was ready. Mr. and Mrs. Rodriguez were surprised that it had taken such a short time to fix all of their problems. They asked the mechanic about the water leak, and he told them that he had just caulked the area of the leak.

As Mr. and Mrs. Rodriguez drove away, they thought of it as a wasted visit. The mechanic had ignored the possibility that the water leak was the result of a structural defect. They felt that the repairs hadn't really fixed anything but were like slapping a bandage on an open, infected wound.

Second Repair Attempt

The leaks and other problems showed up again, forcing Mr. and Mrs. Rodriguez to drive the extra distance to the authorized dealership in Dallas, Texas. They gave the service writer their list of problems, and he put them on a repair order.

The service writer told them it was going to take a while, which proved to be quite an understatement. The motor home was at the dealership for 27 days. During this time, Mr. and Mrs. Rodriguez saw America from a motel in an industrial part of the city. They also had to rent a car.

The Pitfalls of Multiple Warranties

The dealer told Mr. and Mrs. Rodriguez that the handling problem was a chassis issue, and they would have to go to the chassis manufacturer to get it fixed. They called the chassis manufacturer, whose facilities were in another state, and described the problem. The representative said it wasn't their problem; it was the fault of the engine manufacturer.

Motor home components manufacturers
taking responsibility when your vehicle is a lemon.

They called the engine manufacturer, who said it sounded like the weight distribution was incorrect, therefore it was the coach manufacturer's fault. The coach manufacturer took no responsibility for anything, and around and around they went. Meanwhile, the dealership tried more caulk on the leaking roof and fixed a couple of the cosmetic trim problems.

When Mr. and Mrs. Rodriguez finally got back on the road, the handling problem, the roof leak, and the whistling noise from the slide-out were all still present.

Third Repair Attempt

Mr. and Mrs. Rodriguez decided to drive back to the California dealership where they bought the motor home. They would visit friends and relatives while the problems were being fixed.

Motor home owners report that on occasion they have had to use a two-by-four to pry the slideout back into the motor home.

The trip to the dealer was miserable. Once, when they were making a left-hand turn, the slide-out extended on its own, and they barely missed losing the entire slide-out to a passing delivery truck. They had a hard time getting the slide-out to go back in.

At the selling dealer in California, Mr. and Mrs. Rodriguez provided the service writer with their long list of problems, and he put them on a repair order. Most of the items on this repair order had been on earlier repair orders.

Again, the service writer told them it was going to take a while. Again, Mr. and Mrs. Rodriguez were forced to rent a car and stay at a local motel. They had plans to spend Independence Day with friends in Philadelphia, but they had to cancel them. This time the repairs took twenty-two days.

Date: 7/19
Mileage = 6,942
Days in Shop = 22
Total Days in Shop = 52

Fourth Repair Attempt

Soon after the visit to the dealer, Mr. and Mrs. Rodriguez left on a three-day trip to San Diego. On the trip, they discovered that the roof leak hadn't been corrected, the slide-out was causing large cracks in the fiberglass on the outside of the coach, and the handling was as bad as ever.

They decided to try the dealership one more time. Mr. and Mrs. Rodriguez drove back to the dealership through a rain shower, with more water leaking into the motor home. As with the three previous attempts, Mr. and Mrs. Rodriguez provided the service writer with a long list of problems. The service writer put them on a repair order.

The service writer said that it was going to take a while. By this time they knew what that meant. Twenty-five days later the dealership called and said their motor home was ready. It was not. On the first turn out of the dealer's lot, they could feel the handling problem and hear the whistling noise.

Date: 8/16
Mileage = 7,182
Days in Shop = 25
Total Days in Shop = 74

Mr. and Mrs. Rodriguez did not give up or go away. They called an attorney.

A Summary of Motor Home Misery

- The motor home was defective from the moment Mr. and Mrs. Rodriguez took delivery.

- They offered the motor home repeatedly to dealerships and repair facilities for repair.

- The motor home was in the shop for long periods of time without successful repairs. Of the 112 days between May 1 and August 20, the motor home was in for repairs for 74 days.

- None of the manufacturers involved in the construction of the motor home would take responsibility for the defects. Each blamed the other.

- There was a serious safety defect that was never repaired.

CHAPTER 3

A Used Car Lemon Story

> *"To cultivate kindness is a valuable*
> *part of the business of life."*
> —Samuel Johnson

Ms. Peters Bought a Used Car

Ms. Peters was a single mother of three small children and not well off financially. She needed to replace her family's old vehicle because it had finally stopped running altogether. Raising the money for the purchase was difficult.

Ms. Peters went to a local used car dealer and selected a used vehicle that met her needs.

There Was So Much She Didn't Know

The car had an interesting history before Ms. Peters bought it:

A rental car company leased the vehicle, new, early in 1997. This is called the *in-service date,* and is when the new motor vehicle warranty commenced.

Date: 02/15/1997

The car rental company sold the car in February of 1998 to a used car dealer. At that time it had 18,000 miles on the odometer.

Date: 02/21/1998

Date: 02/20/1999

For a while, the used car salesman told potential buyers that the car was a rental, and of course it didn't sell. It stayed on the lot for a year.

This is illegal in California.

Ms. Peters arrived and purchased the car. The salesman did not mention that the car had been a rental.

Used Car Warranties

Ms. Peters received two warranties:

- The dealer provided a 30-day, 1,000-mile bumper-to-bumper warranty that included parts and labor.

- The manufacturer's original new car warranty, which was for 3 years or 36,000 miles, was still in force.

Date: 04/20/1999
Mileage = 18,000

As mentioned, the car had 18,000 miles on the odometer when Ms. Peters purchased it. A balance of 18,000 miles and about eight months remained on the new motor vehicle warranty.

Used Car: First Repair Attempt

Date: 04/24/1999
Mileage = 18,400

As Ms. Peters drove away, she noticed that there was a pronounced engine knock and a pinging noise. She drove the car back to the dealer a few days later. She had driven the car 400 miles.

She tried to impress on them that she was working two jobs and absolutely had to have the car. She described the problem. The service writer said: *"Honey, are you sure you are using the right kind of gas?"*[1]

---

1. See chapter 7, 87, The "Little Lady" Syndrome.

"Honey, are you sure you are using
the right kind of gas?"

He wrote the repair order. She left the car and took the bus to work—several busses, in fact.

Three days later, the dealer called and said the car was ready. The mechanic said that he had checked it over carefully. The repair order said "Engine tune-up." The vehicle's mileage had not changed, showing that there had been no test drive.

Used Car: Second Repair Attempt

Date: 10/25/1999
Mileage = 26,400

The first attempted repair had no effect on the engine knocking and pinging. Ms. Peters also noted that the car didn't seem to have much power. However, it was six months before she could take the car back to the dealer. During those six months, she drove another 8,000 miles.

She told the dealer that the car was doing exactly the same thing she described the first time she brought it in. When she also mentioned the lack of power, the mechanic said, *"Oh, that's the way this model works, dear."* [2] She thought his attitude was patronizing.

Date: 10/30/1999
Mileage = 26,400
Days in Shop = 5
Total Days in Shop = 12

The mechanic wrote a repair order. Five days later he called and said the car was ready. He told Ms. Peters that he had replaced the emission control valve, which was clogged and interfering with the vacuum system. Despite this repair, Ms. Peters noticed no change in the vehicle's performance.

Used Car: Third Repair Attempt

Date: 9/25/2000
Mileage = 36,400

Ten months later, unable to stand the incessant knocking and pinging, Ms. Peters took the car back to the dealer again. She had driven another 10,000 miles. This time the dealer's attitude was contemptuous: *"Oh, you again!"* [3] The mechanic wrote up another repair order. Again Ms. Peters struggled to find transportation to work.

Original Warranty Runs Out

Date: 10/01/2000
Mileage = 36,400
Days in Shop = 6
Total Days in Shop = 18

Six days later the service manager called and said her car was ready. This time they said they had checked everything and couldn't find anything wrong: the repair order read "NPF"—no problem found. As the manufacturer's warranty had expired, the dealer charged her $150 for diagnostic time.

---

2. See chapter 7, 86, That's the Way It Was Designed to Operate.
3. See chapter 7, 90, Dealer Is Intentionally Rude.

As she drove away, the car pinged and knocked as it had from the moment she bought it. She continued to use the car. What else could she do?

Used Car: Fourth Repair Attempt

Nine months later the car became so weak Ms. Peters was afraid to drive it up a hill. It felt like it was going to stall at any moment. Ms. Peters took the vehicle back to the dealer. She pleaded with the mechanic to do something about it, so he took the car and wrote up another repair order.

The car remained in the shop for two weeks. This was very difficult for Ms. Peters. There was considerable additional expense.

Date: 7/01/2001
Mileage = 44,400
Days in Shop = 14
Total Days in Shop = 32

When the service manager called to tell her to pick up the car, she asked what they had found. The service manager said they had found no problem, but that it was time for a tune-up. She had to pay $350 for a tune-up that she hadn't asked for, and that didn't fix the problem.

Used Car: Fifth Repair Attempt

This is a condition called *dieseling.*

The car continued to knock and ping. When Ms. Peters turned off the engine, it kept running, making a terrible racket.

Eleven months later, she was again able to take the car to the dealer. The service manager was standing there when she drove up. After she shut off the engine, it continued to run, knocking and pinging loudly. This time the service manager didn't make any snide remarks but just wrote up the repair order. Once again, Ms. Peters arranged for a ride home.

Date: 06/01/2002
Mileage = 56,501

Date: 07/08/2002
Mileage = 56,501
Days in Shop = 7
Total Days in Shop = 39

A week later, the service manager called to say her car was ready to pick up. He said he had checked everything, performed a full service, and put some special anti-knock oil in her car. The dealer presented another bill for $350.00. As she drove away, the pinging and lack of power were unchanged. If Ms. Peters had had the money to buy a different car, she would have.

Used Car: Sixth Repair Attempt

Date: 05/03/2003
Mileage = 66,501
Days in Shop = 8
Total Days in Shop = 47

Date: 05/11/2003

Ten months later, she found time to take the car to the dealership again for the same problems. The mechanic took the car and wrote the repair order. She got another tune-up, which didn't solve anything; the car spent another eight days in the shop, and the dealer presented a bill for $350.00.

She Went to an Attorney

Ms. Peters had had enough, but she couldn't afford to give up and go away. A few days after picking up her car, she looked in the telephone directory and found an attorney specializing in lemon law.

A Summary of the Used Car Story

- The dealership failed to disclose to Ms. Peters that the vehicle was a rental car.

- The defect was present when she purchased the vehicle.

- She first returned the car for repairs while it was still covered by both warranties.

- The vehicle was in the shop for more than thirty days, and six repair attempts.

- Because Ms. Peters wasn't able to bring in the car very often, the failed repair attempts dragged on for more than four years.[4]

The dealership treated Ms. Peters's problems as a maintenance issue. They never once diagnosed the real cause of the vehicle's problems.

4. See chapter 11, 148, Statute of Limitations.

PART 2

Why We Need
Lemon Laws

CHAPTER 4

A Brief History of Lemon Law

> *"Human history becomes more and more a race between education and catastrophe."*
> —H. G. Wells, *The Outline of History*

In the Beginning There Was Commercial Chaos

There have always been those who would sell you an ox cart made from rotting wood with wheels shaped like footballs. Warranty law is by no means a new thing, but it has been slow in developing.

AD 1250: St. Thomas Aquinas Weighs In

In his *Summa Theologica,* Thomas Aquinas (Saint Thomas) wrote an extraordinarily lucid set of definitions that neatly divided defective goods into three types:

1. A seller did not need to mention a *manifest flaw* to the buyer. Although the seller would exhibit *the more exuberant virtue* by disclosure, Aquinas agreed with the ancient adage *"A buyer's eye is his merchant where the defect is obvious."*

2. If the defect was latent—that is, discovered some time after the sale—and unknown to either the buyer or the seller, then the seller was still required to make good the buyer's loss. (This was an early implied warranty of merchantability.)[1]

---

1. See chapter 9, 120, Implied Warranties.

3. If the defect was latent but known to the seller at the time of sale (and not to the buyer), then the sale was void and the seller was *guilty of sin.*

1603: England, Caveat Emptor

A lemon vehicle in the 21st century is something like a 17th-century bezoar stone. However, like the stone in *Chandelor v. Lopus,* the magic is missing.

Unfortunately, merchants paid little heed to Saint Thomas Aquinas's rules for responsible sellers, following instead another doctrine: *caveat emptor,* or *let the buyer beware.* Legal historians place the first formal application of the concept in the 1603 case of *Chandelor v. Lopus.* In that case, the seller sold what he claimed was a *bezoar* stone said to have magical healing properties. Strangely enough, the stone turned out not to be the real thing, so the buyer sued.

The buyer made no showing that the seller knew the stone was a fake when he sold it. Under medieval doctrine, the seller would have been liable for the problem anyway, because it would have been considered a latent defect in the stone without the knowledge of either party. However, the court hearing the case refused to undo the sale, holding the buyer responsible for his own decision to purchase what he believed was a magical stone without any express warranty.

The court held that a seller would not be responsible in the absence of either (1) knowledge of the truth, which would be fraud if not disclosed, or (2) an explicit express warranty from the seller that the object was in fact a magical stone. Merely saying that the stone was magical, without guaranteeing it, was not enough. Although the court did not use the phrase *caveat emptor,* its conclusion was plain enough.

1906: The Uniform Sales Act

When the United States broke away from England, they kept her legal system. Even today, forty-nine of the fifty states base their laws on the old English *common law*. (Louisana bases its legal system on a blend of English common law and French civil law.) Still, each state's laws are different.

The Uniform Sales Act of 1906 was an attempt to regulate commerce in the United States. This was the time of the great robber barons who banded together to monopolize commodities in their area so that they could manipulate prices and profits. There was great need for regulation.

The Uniform Sales Act was one of several uniform laws intended to minimize the differences in laws between the states. Each state had the option to write its own statutes, adopting all, some, or none of each uniform act to fit the particular state. The hope was that, where several states enacted the same provision of a uniform act, their interpretations of that provision would be consistent.

1952: A Uniform Commercial Code (U.C.C.)

Eventually the National Conference of Commissioners on Uniform State Laws realized there was a need to update the existing statutes. In 1940, the president of the conference first proposed the idea of a Uniform Commercial Code to replace seven of the older uniform acts, including the Uniform Sales Act, and to bring the laws of commerce up to date.

The U.C.C.'s focus on commercial transactions seriously limits its use to consumers.

The first official U.C.C. emerged in 1952, after more than ten years of drafting and revisions. Substantial revisions and amendments followed over the next several years, until finally in 1961 the National Conference decided to establish a Permanent Editorial Board for the Uniform Commercial Code. The board released its official text of the U.C.C. in 1962. Since then, forty-nine states have enacted some form of the U.C.C.—all except Lousiana.

The purpose of the U.C.C. was to simplify, clarify, and modernize the law governing commerce and trade, and to standardize commercial law among the various states. Thus, the U.C.C. applies primarily to commercial transactions between commercial parties.

The U.C.C. was not designed for consumers as much as it was for merchants. It does not take into account the unique realities of consumer purchases. It does not provide sufficient protection for consumers. California was one of the first states to address this problem, and to this day California still has one of the country's strongest lemon laws.

1970: Song-Beverly Consumer Warranty Act

Laws that benefit the individual inevitably come under attack by corporate interests. Somewhere between the needs of both there is fairness.

Under California's Song-Beverly Consumer Warranty Act, manufacturers are entitled only to a *reasonable number of attempts* to repair defective consumer goods. If manufacturers or their agents are unsuccessful, they must either replace the goods or refund the purchase price. This is the basic remedy that nearly all lemon laws now provide.

The Song-Beverly Act is also meant to make it economically viable for consumers to bring warranty suits, by providing for an award of attorneys' fees.[2] The law bears the name of its authors in the California legislature, Alfred H. Song and Robert G. Beverly.

---

2. See chapter 12, 160, Attorneys' Fees: Can I Afford to Sue?

Without the lemon law, Mr. and Mrs. Jones were in a David and Goliath contest where all the weapons favored Goliath.

1975: Federal Lemon Law

In 1975, Congress enacted the Magnuson-Moss Warranty–Federal Trade Commission Improvement Act. While it was not as effective as California's Song-Beverly Act, the federal Magnuson-Moss Act did attempt to encourage warrantors to provide better warranties. It also included a provision allowing—but not requiring—courts to award attorneys' fees to consumers who had to file lawsuits to enforce warranties.

The great equalizer: courts could compel manufacturers to reimburse attorneys' fees.

Congress established guidelines for mechanisms to attempt to resolve warranty disputes without litigation. California later added similar guidelines to the Song-Beverly Act, and other states have also followed suit.

1982: The Tanner Consumer Protection Act

Substantial
impairment to
use, value, or
safety is defined.

California Assemblywoman Sally Tanner first intro-
duced this key measure in 1980. The Tanner Act
is part of the Song-Beverly Act, but its provisions
apply specifically to motor vehicles. The law defines
guidelines for a *reasonable number* of repair attempts.[3]
It also defines *nonconformity* to mean a nonconformity
that substantially impairs the use, value, or safety of
the motor vehicle to the buyer or lessee.

The Tanner Act has become the model for lemon laws in
other states. Today, all fifty states have enacted lemon
laws. It is no accident that all of these state legislatures,
as well as Congress, have found it necessary to protect
citizens in this way.

1991: Automotive Consumer Notification Act

California was at
the cutting edge
of consumer
advocacy again.

This Act was added to California's lemon law to
reduce what is known as *lemon laundering*.[4] Some
auto manufacturers were trying to resell the lemons
they repurchased to unsuspecting used car buyers. To
prevent this, manufacturers are now required to *brand*
the titles of defective vehicles to indicate that they are
lemon law buybacks.

Before reselling a lemon law buyback, manufacturers
are required to do the following:

- Submit the vehicle's title to the
  Department of Motor Vehicles for
  branding

- Affix a permanent decal to the vehicle
  itself, indicating that it was a lemon law
  buyback

---

3. See chapter 8, 99, "How Can I Tell If My Vehicle Is a Lemon?"
4. See chapter 13, 169, "Lemon Laundering."

- Disclose that the vehicle was repurchased due to defects

- Disclose what repairs were performed to correct the defects

- Provide a one-year warranty to the next consumer

This addition to the law was particularly needed when a consumer was purchasing a used vehicle that the dealer asserted was free of defects. The consumer might never discover that the vehicle had been declared a lemon in another state and then shipped to California for resale.

CHAPTER 5

The Need for Lemon Law

*"The soul of a corporation should emulate
the soul of a man at his best,
not his worst."*
—Donald P. Ladew

Introduction to the Need for Lemon Law

People can make all the negative comments they like about there being too many laws, but countries without these protections are sorry places to live. True, if every manufacturer always stood behind its products unconditionally, there would be no need for lemon laws. Instead, every state in the union has some kind of lemon law to protect its citizens from living with defective vehicles. This confirms that there is a need to protect consumers. Manufacturers left to their own devices will not do the right thing.

By itself, a defective automobile might seem like a small thing. It is certainly not as significant as war, famine, or the injustices done to whole peoples. However, as an example of a national corporate disease in an industrial age, it is not a small thing. It is no accident that so many people find themselves with a lemon. For every effect, there is a cause.

The need for any set of laws to control corporate behavior speaks poorly of the individuals in charge. But for the consumer to be without these laws would at best lead to an incredible waste of time and money, and at worst prove hazardous to life and limb.

The Right Way to Handle a Defect

When manufacturers produce defective vehicles that they cannot repair, reason and ethics suggest that they should acknowledge the defect, replace the vehicle, and get on with their business, taking pains to correct the defect in later models.

Common sense says that this is the essence of correct corporate behavior:

- Determine that you have made a mistake

- Take responsibility for it

- Correct the situation

This is the sort of behavior our fathers and mothers told us would make a worthwhile, decent adult. This should not be an unrealistic goal, for people and corporations alike.

Sears, for example, has a policy of "Satisfaction guaranteed or your money back." It is certainly logical for a retailer to take responsibility for the products it sells, rather than to inflict the consequences of its mistakes on the unsuspecting customers. The next logical step is for the retailer to go to the original suppliers of the defective goods and compel them to improve the quality of their products. It seems the sensible solution.

The Real World

Corporate responsibility is the way things should be, but it is not the way things are. Instead of taking responsibility for their products, many companies just pass on to their customers their failure to monitor and improve quality. Automobile manufacturer irresponsibility is a primary reason why consumers need the protection of lemon laws. There was a great need to level the playing field, and those who framed these laws knew it.

Quantity vs. Quality

Manufacturers, particularly in the United States, have lost their focus on the true meaning of a quality product: a finished, high-quality article in the hands of the consumer in exchange for a fair price.

In America we salute quantity and pay lip service to quality. When manufacturers want to brag, they cite numbers of units produced, tons of ore mined, miles of cable laid, or millions of books sold. People involved in high production get bonuses, gold-plated plaques, and vacations in Las Vegas.

While production managers are enjoying these perks, quality managers are instead trying to get people to attend classes on process improvement, trying to get a budget to buy inspection tools, and fighting with the production managers to maintain standards. The quality supervisor has no vacations to give her people; she buys *Quality Award Certificates* for her people from Office Depot and fills them in herself.

> Manufacturers win the quantity battle and we lose the quality war.

W. Edwards Deming: The Quality Revolution

It is a sad commentary on American industry's regard for quality that an American was most responsible for the "quality revolution" in Japan, yet he was ignored in America for years. Dr. W. Edwards Deming, a statistician, worked with the United States military during World War II to improve manufacturing production. His primary focus was on quality, which he defined as a product's ability to conform to the customer's requirements. He also insisted on a constant, measurable improvement of quality.

Dr. Deming wrote: "Learning is not compulsory; neither is survival."

Dr. Deming taught that the best way to improve production was to improve quality. He was so successful that in 1950, after the war, the Japanese government invited him to teach their scientists and engineers. The Japanese knew that, without any natural resources except people, they had to do something to be able to manufacture goods that could be sold to world markets.

The figure below is at the heart of what Dr. Deming taught. He called it a *quality chain reaction,* and he put it on the blackboard at every meeting with Japanese engineers.

Figure 5.1. A Quality Chain Reaction

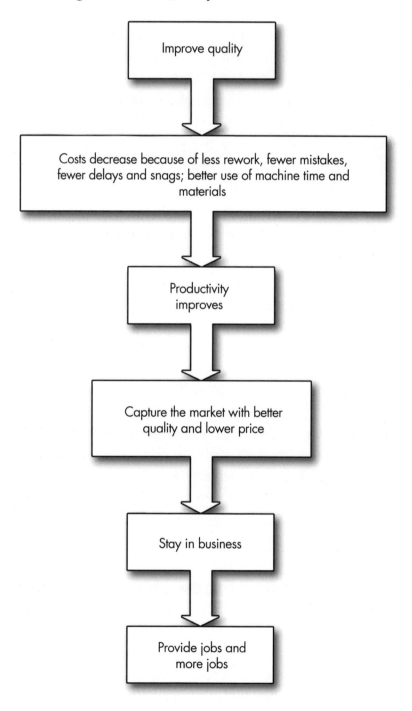

The Japanese paid excellent attention to Dr. Deming and applied what they learned. We live with the results of how well they applied this knowledge. In every quality survey, Japanese automobiles appear at the top. Go to any store for every imaginable kind of goods, and Japanese products are there. It isn't an accident.

Dr. Deming and American Manufacturers

During the 1980s, when American businesses finally realized the threat to their markets, American industry invited Dr. Deming to teach them what he had taught the Japanese. Some companies learned, and they are still reaping the rewards of a focus on quality.

Among Dr. Deming's many clients were General Motors and Ford. Their personnel had the same opportunity as the Japanese engineers who went on to design and build vehicles for Toyota, Honda, Mazda, and Datsun (now Nissan). Did they take advantage of that opportunity? A cursory look at the results of any recent automotive "Initial Quality Survey" from J.D. Power and Associates makes it apparent that they did not.[1]

How did American businesses miss this opportunity? Dr. Deming urged them to focus on quality. Instead, they chose to focus on quantity. They chose to focus on the quarterly report to shareholders.

The Chain of Modern Economics

The publicly held corporation in America lives and dies by its quarterly financial report. The quarterly report drives the value of the stock. Every corporate decision, every management choice, good or bad, is based on its effect on the quarterly report. That's only three months! In contrast, the typical Japanese company bases its plans on one-, five-, twenty-, and even fifty-year cycles. That's right, fifty!

---

1. Refer to J.D. Power's Web-site link in appendix B, Bibliography.

When the American corporate eye looks no further than three months into the future, it is not surprising that business planning is defensive rather than forward-looking. This philosophy produces disasters like Enron. Although it may be difficult to believe, it is also why Mr. and Mrs. Jones fought a year-long battle to get justice after purchasing a lemon vehicle.[2]

Quality is held hostage to the quarterly report. When the quarterly report looks bad, training, services, and quality departments are the first to suffer reductions in budget. Self-serving commercial practices ensue, and the customer is forced to live with the result.

Management Ethics and Greed

When a company's directors worry about the condition of the stock, they seldom accept responsibility for their part in the process. They don't look at what their demands on management have caused.

The combined salaries and perks of the top ten people at Ford and GM can be greater than the gross national product of a small country. Such disproportionate salaries could never exist without the agreement of the board of directors, and, by extension, of every stockholder.

Is it wrong for these executives to make a nice living? No, it is not. But their huge salaries and perks are paid at the expense of Mr. and Mrs. Jones's year-long misery. Corporate resources are not infinite, and every $250,000 going to an executive means that much less going to maintain the quality of the company's products.

2. See chapter 1, 3, "A New Car Lemon Story."

The Yardstick of Success Is Wrong

The average executive plans for a two- to three-year stay in a particular assignment. He or she has no incentive to implement a long-term continuing improvement of quality. Although companies may pay lip service to quality, there are no serious rewards for reducing the number of defective automobiles produced or diminishing the number of recalls.

The goal of every chief executive in America is the improvement of production numbers, the improvement of the quarterly financial report, the improvement of the bottom line. They are rewarded for increasing quantity, not quality. What the management of American automobile manufacturers has failed to understand is that this shortsighted viewpoint can be painfully expensive.

Figure 5.2. The Cost of Manufacturing a Lemon Vehicle

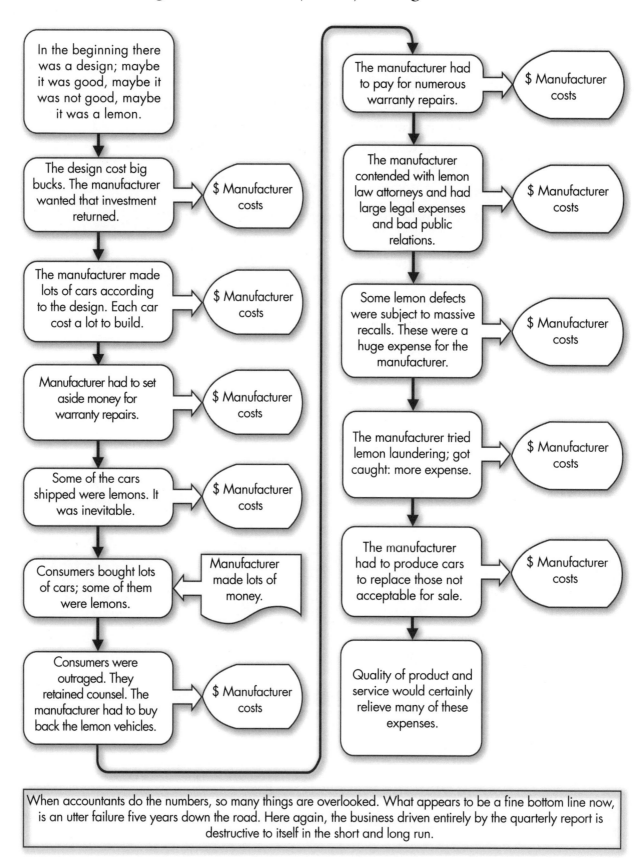

In the beginning there was a design; maybe it was good, maybe it was not good, maybe it was a lemon.

The design cost big bucks. The manufacturer wanted that investment returned.

$ Manufacturer costs

The manufacturer made lots of cars according to the design. Each car cost a lot to build.

$ Manufacturer costs

Manufacturer had to set aside money for warranty repairs.

$ Manufacturer costs

Some of the cars shipped were lemons. It was inevitable.

$ Manufacturer costs

Consumers bought lots of cars; some of them were lemons.

Manufacturer made lots of money.

Consumers were outraged. They retained counsel. The manufacturer had to buy back the lemon vehicles.

$ Manufacturer costs

The manufacturer had to pay for numerous warranty repairs.

$ Manufacturer costs

The manufacturer contended with lemon law attorneys and had large legal expenses and bad public relations.

$ Manufacturer costs

Some lemon defects were subject to massive recalls. These were a huge expense for the manufacturer.

$ Manufacturer costs

The manufacturer tried lemon laundering; got caught: more expense.

$ Manufacturer costs

The manufacturer had to produce cars to replace those not acceptable for sale.

$ Manufacturer costs

Quality of product and service would certainly relieve many of these expenses.

When accountants do the numbers, so many things are overlooked. What appears to be a fine bottom line now, is an utter failure five years down the road. Here again, the business driven entirely by the quarterly report is destructive to itself in the short and long run.

Top Executives Set Standards of Corporations

So far, I have tried to give you a small part of a bigger picture, something that can help you to come to grips with what may seem hard to comprehend. Why do you spend $30,000 of your hard-earned money on a car, only to have it inexplicably stall in traffic, scaring you and your family half to death? It starts at the top of the corporation.

Vehicle manufacturers cannot be depended on to exercise self-discipline. Instead, it is up to society to establish a system of laws, and enforce them rigorously, in order to maintain balance and fair play.

President of the United States Harry S. Truman had a sign on his desk that said The Buck Stops Here. He knew that ultimately responsibility flows to the top and stops there.

Volume of Defective Consumer Goods

Despite the problems I have discussed, quality in America is considerably better today than it was twenty years ago. Individual components are often subjected to more rigorous quality testing. As a result, more defects are caught before the final product is assembled. Unfortunately, these advances are more than offset by the extraordinary complexity of the modern automobile.

If fewer lemons were being manufactured, perhaps there wouldn't be such a great need for lemon laws. However, every statistical survey of quality—this is borne out by the number of lemon law buybacks occurring every year—suggests that the number of defective vehicles being produced has not declined. If anything, it is on the increase. The question isn't whether lemons are being produced, but how many?

How Many Lemons?

It is estimated that California car dealers sell 1,500,000 new motor vehicles per year. Various studies have found that an alarming percentage of vehicles manufactured in any given year turn out to be lemons. One such study in the late eighties estimated the percentage to be as high as 10 percent.[3] This means at one time there may have been as many as 150,000 new lemons on the road in California alone! Even if the percentage were only 1 percent, 15,000 lemon vehicles every year, in just one state, is still a serious problem. Nothing we have seen indicates that these numbers have been reduced over the intervening twenty years.

Complexity and Malfunctions: A Catch-22

Let's look at the increasing complexity of the modern automobile. All manufacturers want to gain an edge over the competition. They need to tell consumers that their vehicles offer more and better conveniences. These lead to greater complexity, and greater complexity increases the number of parts.

When there are more parts, there are simply more things that can go wrong. This increases the possibility that a car will become a lemon—even if each individual part is of higher overall quality. If only one out of every thousand components is defective, a car with 15,000 components will still have five times as many defects as a car with 3,000 components.

A part that works properly 99.9 percent of the time will still fail one time in 1,000. Put together just fifty parts that work properly 99.9 percent of the time, and the entire vehicle will work properly only 95.2 percent of the time—failing nearly one time in twenty. What do you think happens when manufacturers assemble 15,000 parts?

---

3. Refer to appendix B, *Lemon Law: A Manual for Consumers.*

It isn't difficult to see that producing lemon vehicles is inevitable. Indeed, it is in part a problem of our own making. Manufacturers put things in vehicles that consumers demand, and that will give the manufacturers the sales edge. Thus, you and I are partially responsible for the increased complexity that leads to lemons.

Unless there is a fundamental change in vehicle design, cars, trucks, motor homes, and motorcycles are not going to become any less complex.

Example of Fundamental Change in Technology:

How many parts are there in a modern automobile? Five hundred? A thousand? It's closer to fifteen thousand! By contrast, a hydrogen-oxygen fuel cell electric power plant, still fifteen to twenty years in the future, has two outputs, electricity and water, and it has no moving parts larger than an electron. And you can drink the water!

Complexity and Quality

We have been looking at two factors: complexity and defects. The added dimension is quality. Japanese manufacturing is an excellent example. Are there more parts in a Lexus than in an equivalent model Mercedes? Both are equally complex, yet Mercedes vehicles have far more problems than Lexus vehicles.[4] The power of quality, applied rigorously throughout the manufacturing process, can utterly transform what seems like a statistical certainty.

---

4. Refer to J.D. Power Initial Quality Surveys Web-site link in appendix B.

Automobile Complexity in the Computer Age

Each year, cars, trucks, boats, and RVs get more complicated. In this new electronic world, computers manage most of the various vehicle operations, such as powertrain, transmission, brake systems, emission control system, and safety related systems, to list a few.

Figure 5.3. Typical Vehicle Computer (ECU)

Here's a software truism: Garbage in, Garbage out (GIGO). If you stuff a half million lines of software code into a vehicle computer, the chance that some part of it is garbage increases significantly. Maybe that bad line of code is what makes your car lunge at stop signs, scaring you and your passengers half to death.

In twenty years we have gone from a completely mechanical automobile—no electronics—to vehicles that have as many as forty or fifty computers, controlling everything from acceleration to tire pressure. This sort of accelerated development has a price. Unlike your desktop PC, there is no standardization in vehicle computers, either software or hardware. Often nothing in the software is common from manufacturer to manufacturer, or even model to model.

This lack of standardization is bad for everyone. The mechanic is in trouble because he hasn't been trained to use the sophisticated new diagnostic tools. The owner pays a heavy price because when a computer fails, finding the exact cause can be very difficult. Thus, the owner waits, often for weeks or even months, for the dealership to figure out what is wrong.

Figure 5.4. Typical Vehicle Computer Systems

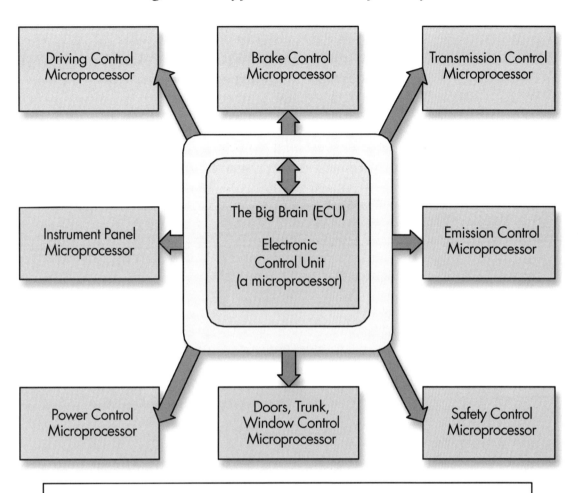

The main Electronic Control Unit and all the microprocessors that deal with specific vehicle systems are not independent. They talk to each other in diverse and complex ways. When something goes wrong in the main computer, the effects may be felt broadly throughout the affected vehicle.

The dealership is caught between the demands of high warranty repair expense and the need to service the customer. And, finally, the manufacturer is under pressure to maintain the appearance of manufacturing cars that do everything advertised perfectly.

Customers want more sexy gadgets. There's a price: added complexity.

Manufacturers compete in a tough business environment, so they must offer new and sexy gadgets to the consumer. Customers ask for these things and if the manufacturer doesn't provide them, the competition will.

The move toward more and more computerization in cars, trucks, boats, and RVs is driven by a need for the following:

- Sophisticated engine control systems to meet emissions and fuel-economy standards

- Advanced troubleshooting diagnostics

- Simplification of manufacture and design

- Reduction of wiring (less wiring equals less weight, which equals better gas mileage)

- Management of sophisticated new safety features

- Control of comfort and convenience features

- Increased competition in a tough business environment

The need for simplification in manufacturing and design was brought to the fore in an article on the front page of the May 31, 2004, issue of *Automotive News*, titled "Mercedes ditches glitches with electronics." The article speaks clearly about the problems of too much technology. Because of serious problems with defects, Mercedes is removing six hundred electronic functions from its vehicles.

A recent review of lemon vehicle legal cases indicated that a remarkably high percentage had major defects that were directly or indirectly related to one or more of the on-board computers. When something goes wrong with an automobile, manufacturers want to talk about individual components, but not the part of the vehicle that tells the components how to operate: the on-board computer.

Typically the manufacturer will talk about an emission control valve failing, not about the Electronic Control Unit (a microprocessor) and its subordinate system the Emission Control Computer (another microprocessor) that tells the emission control valve when and how to work.

Another issue that prevents customers from getting excellent service is knowledge—or, rather, lack of knowledge. For the average mechanic, these computers are a new and fearful thing. They know that if they fool around with anything that has a computer in it, they are going to mess up and get in big trouble. In an article on BMW fuel injection fault codes— these are the codes the Engine Control Computer generates indicating what is wrong with a particular system—the master mechanic who wrote the article described the task of retrieving and understanding the control codes as being very difficult: "It's a one on a scale of one to ten, one being most difficult."

What if there is a software design fault? Or what if there is a basic computer hardware design fault within the computer itself? Now, the manufacturer could be looking at possible recalls.

Still, the dealer has to get the work done; so, inexperienced mechanics are put to work on problems they do not understand and really do not want to do. Who bears the brunt of their lack of training, aptitude, and attitude? Right again, the long-suffering consumer.

There is a nationwide shortage of trained mechanics, so severe that dealers and repair shops recruit from prisons in the Midwest. None of these conditions bode well for the consumer.

Every microprocessor in the modern automobile has multiple sensor inputs. Sensors measure things like engine temperature, rpm, vehicle speed, and so on. Sensors may be variable, collecting changing values, like vehicle speed, which the computer uses to make decisions, or they may be looking at the output of switches that are simply on or off.

The Engine Control Computer may be connected to fifty or more of these microprocessors and hundreds of sensors. Nevertheless, very few of these sensors, if defective, will produce one isolated fault code. The failure of these sensors to operate properly at the proper time can create a multitude of hard-to-diagnose problems. Some of these problems present a serious safety hazard to the owner.

When the brain of a vehicle is defective, its effects may be seen throughout the body of the vehicle.

It's not a simple thing when the *brain* of a vehicle, or a human, is defective. Like a cancer, it spreads out into other systems and affects them in unpredictable ways. It is a tough situation, and manufacturers and dealerships do not improve it by denying that such problems exist.

It is thoughtless and possibly worse for a dealership to replace the emission control valve when your car begins to stall, and then tell you that everything is all right. A week later, when it stalls in an intersection, the dealer will find some other component. But the dealer is just treating the symptoms, not addressing the real cause. It is similar to a surgeon replacing your arm because the brain isn't sending it the right commands for proper operation.

One answer, of course, is more rigorous testing of its products by the manufacturer. Mandatory programs to upgrade the skills of mechanics would also go a long way toward improving service, safety, and the vehicle ownership experience. Until then, consumers will continue to suffer the consequences of overly complex vehicles.

How Many People Just Give Up?

If lemon vehicles are produced at even one-tenth of the numbers mentioned earlier, how many of their owners take on the manufacturers or the dealerships, and finally get replacements or refunds for their defective cars?

For every consumer who tries to reject his or her vehicle, there are probably fifteen more who are trying to drive to work, get the children to school, and do all the other driving that a family does in a year, all in a vehicle that has substantially impaired use, value, and safety—that is, is a lemon.

With the corporate model described in this chapter firmly in place, it is essential that consumers find protection in the law. This book is my attempt to ensure that the consumer has access to the information needed to level the playing field.

Consumers Have No Idea That They Have Rights

> Most consumers have no idea that they have rights under the law. Even if they do, they erroneously believe that they cannot afford to hire an attorney to take their case. Nothing could be further from the truth.

Consumers can seek legal help anytime they want. Manufacturers and dealerships have no say in this.

"I guess we're not the only ones with a lemon, Sandy."

CHAPTER 6

Manufacturer-Dealership Relationship

> *"Third prize is you're fired."*
> —David Mamet, *Glengarry GlenRoss*

It's a Business Relationship

The Manufacturer-Dealership relationship is a business relationship. Automobile dealerships are big businesses, and becoming more so as economic pressures force more and more dealers to consolidate. This is the age of the megadealership.

The manufacturer has a contract with the dealership. The dealership gets a license from the manufacturer to sell its vehicles and repair them under warranty. This contract sets out the rules of the relationship.

Risk and Reward: The Games Manufacturers Play

In American business, the bottom line is profit. Both manufacturers and dealerships must make money. Many things can interfere with this goal. Consider the following situations, which create overwhelming pressure on the dealership:

- The manufacturer is producing large numbers of defective products. The dealer can't change this.

- The manufacturer sets a warranty repair budget for the dealership. When the budget is depleted, the dealership is penalized. For example, the dealership may have to eat repair costs.

A vehicle is not necessarily a lemon just because something is wrong with it. It would be hard to find a car, motor home, or boat these days that doesn't have something wrong with it.

- The manufacturer also creates a variety of bonus programs for dealers, based not on quality of product or service but on staying within the warranty repair budget. When the budget is exceeded, these bonuses are withheld from the dealership's management.

- Manufacturers create games where the "winner" is the dealership with the lowest number of hours billed for warranty repairs over the game period, typically a month or a business quarter. This kind of incentive drives dealerships to cut corners.

- Manufacturers create arbitrary time limits for warranty repairs. The dealership and its technicians have no incentive to take their time with repairs. Indeed, they have every incentive to go as fast as possible.

A vehicle is not a lemon just because it has a defect, **but because it cannot be fixed**. Manufacturers are responsible for the original defects, but the foregoing and other practices create an environment that actually discourages dealers from properly repairing vehicles under warranty.

Warranty Repair Budgets

Part of the contract between a manufacturer and a dealer lets the manufacturer select a warranty repair budget. The manufacturer unilaterally limits the dollar amount of warranty repairs for which it will reimburse the dealer, per month or per quarter. When this budget is exceeded, the dealership must absorb additional warranty repair costs.

Dealerships cannot afford to treat these losses lightly, or to exceed their warranty repair budget every month. This is big business, and dealers make an average of 11–12 percent of their net profits on service repairs.[1] But they still have to sell the products the manufacturer sends them, even if they are defective.

Secret Warranties

What happens when defects in certain vehicle models become known? For safety-related defects, the National Highway Traffic Safety Administration can order what is called a *recall*. Many times, manufacturers will conduct a recall voluntarily—sometimes even before NHTSA gets involved. Whether a recall is voluntary or compulsory, the manufacturer must do several things:

1. The manufacturer must arrange to repair the defect at no charge, or, if the manufacturer chooses, to replace or repurchase the vehicle or defective component.

2. The manufacturer must file a public report, which must contain the following information:

    - The defect

    - The types of vehicles or equipment affected

    - The major events that led to the recall

    - The remedy the manufacturer will provide

    - The schedule for the recall

---

1. Refer to http://www.naa.org/artpage.cfm?AID=2925&SID=5.

3.   The manufacturer must send a written notice to all owners of the affected vehicles, containing the following data:

- The defect

- The particular risk or hazard that the defect creates

- The remedy available, including when it will be available and how long it will take

- What the owners can do if they have any trouble getting the recall accomplished in a reasonable time without charge

4.   When the owners bring in the affected vehicles, the manufacturer must pay for the repair or other remedy.

5.   The manufacturer must make the repairs regardless of whether the warranty is still in effect, usually up until the vehicle is ten years old.

6.   If some owners have already had the defect repaired at their own expense, the manufacturer usually must reimburse them.

Recalls can affect hundreds of thousands of vehicles and cost the manufacturer tens of millions of dollars. Beyond even these extraordinary costs is the damage done to the manufacturer's reputation. Needless to say, manufacturers will do almost anything to avoid a recall.

Whatever You Do, Hide the Recall

A *secret warranty* is a strategy that manufacturers use to avoid a recall. Under a secret warranty, manufacturers will pay for repair of a particular defect in a particular kind of vehicle, even after the warranty has expired—but only for those consumers who are sufficiently aggressive in their complaints. *The squeaky wheel gets the grease.*

Manufacturers issue secret warranties in response to defects that have occurred in a widespread pattern—defects that may otherwise lead to recalls. Manufacturers call them *warranty adjustment policies* or *goodwill gestures*. In the trade, they are called *secret warranties* because they are communicated only to the company's regional offices and dealers, but never to consumers.

How Do I Find Out About a Secret Warranty?

Good luck! They are usually very difficult to discover, and manufacturers often deny the existence of secret warranties.

To find a *secret warranty*, check through the TSBs for your model vehicle that authorize the dealer to make repairs at the manufacturer's expense.

You can start by checking the Technical Service Bulletins[2] (TSBs) at your dealer's office for your vehicle model and year. The existence of a TSB does not necessarily mean that the manufacturer has a secret warranty. It does signal that the manufacturer is aware of a recurring, widespread defect or problem.

Although TSBs can be hard to decipher, the key is to find one that authorizes the dealer to make repairs at the manufacturer's expense, even when the defect is not covered under warranty. Watch for code words such as *Check for availability of goodwill assistance.*

2. Check the Alldata Web site at www.alldata.com.

"All cars run a little rough sometimes, Mr. Jones.
Not to worry, we'll tune it up for you."

You can also ask your dealer if the repairs for a certain defect are covered by a *warranty adjustment policy*. If this fails, contact the manufacturer's regional office and ask the same question.

Is Disclosure of Secret Warranties Required?

A very few states, including California, require manufacturers to

- notify by mail all owners affected by a warranty adjustment policy;

- make available upon request the applicable TSBs;

- provide for reimbursement to consumers who have already paid for the covered repair.

Don't depend on manufacturers to do this voluntarily. Sometimes they "forget."

Remember, the squeaky wheel gets the grease. If you don't ask about these things, the manufacturer will never tell you voluntarily.

The Flat-Rate Pay System for Technicians

The vast majority of dealerships in the United States pay their technicians according to a *flat-rate* pay system.

- *Service Labor Time Standards* are how Ford determines the length of time that should be spent on any warranty or recall repair. All car manufacturers have some similar method of determining how long they think a particular repair should take.

- Manufacturers print labor time manuals. These manuals define warranty repair time standards for every possible kind of repair.

- Time standards are set for each job and are rounded to the nearest tenth of an hour. For instance, the standard for replacement of an ignition module on a particular car may be 1.1 hours. This means that, no matter how long it takes the technician to change that module, the manufacturer pays for 1.1 hours.

Under any flat-rate pay system, the technician's entire focus is on getting the repair completed faster than the assigned time.

> The manufacturer's assignment of these times is a serious bone of contention for dealerships and technicians alike.

The manipulation of these times represents extraordinary sums of money. Needless to say, the benefit is to the manufacturer, not the dealer or the consumer.

The manufacturer wants the flat rates to be as low as possible. This is particularly true where there is a potential recall. Ford, for example, has lowered flat rates when it needed to improve its bottom line.[3]

A Recall Example

Recall #99M06 affected 566,979 Ford Contours.

- The labor time before the recall was 0.9 hours.

- The reduced time set by Ford was 0.4 hours.

- This totals 0.5 hours that Ford removed from the time previously allowed for the recall repair.

- Average shop rate is $60.00/hour.

- 566,979 vehicles multiplied by 0.5 hours equals 283,489 hours saved.

- The recall savings to the manufacturer was $60.00 multiplied by 283,489, or **$17,009,340.00**.

- With one stroke of Ford's pen, every dealer involved in these recall repairs lost its portion of $17,009,340.00.

The flat-rate pay system may seem unfair to dealers and their technicians, but that's nothing compared to its effect on consumers.

3. Refer to www.dealer-magazine.com.

Figure 6.1. The Flat-Rate System: A Recipe for Disaster

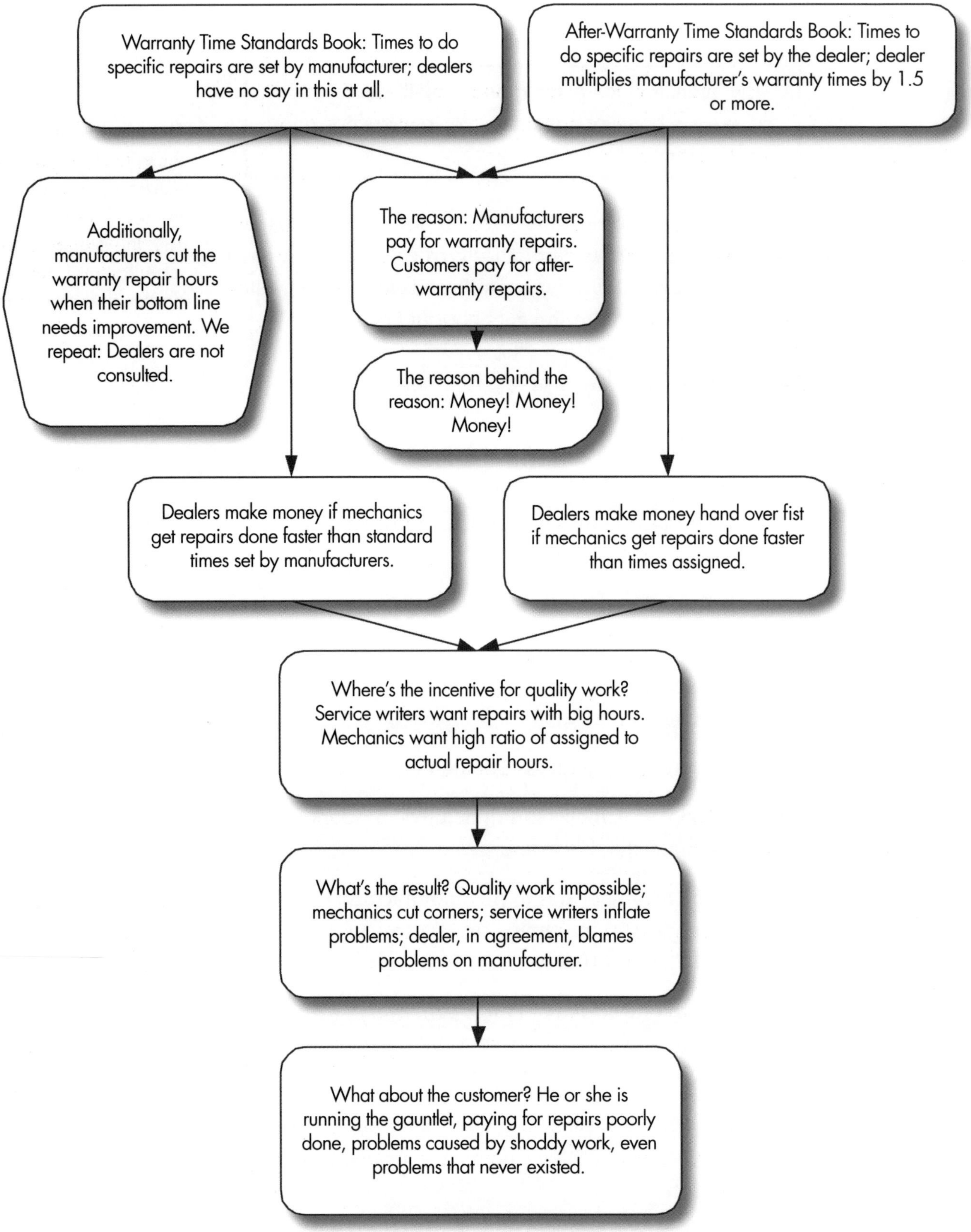

Warranty Time Standards Book: Times to do specific repairs are set by manufacturer; dealers have no say in this at all.

After-Warranty Time Standards Book: Times to do specific repairs are set by the dealer; dealer multiplies manufacturer's warranty times by 1.5 or more.

Additionally, manufacturers cut the warranty repair hours when their bottom line needs improvement. We repeat: Dealers are not consulted.

The reason: Manufacturers pay for warranty repairs. Customers pay for after-warranty repairs.

The reason behind the reason: Money! Money! Money!

Dealers make money if mechanics get repairs done faster than standard times set by manufacturers.

Dealers make money hand over fist if mechanics get repairs done faster than times assigned.

Where's the incentive for quality work? Service writers want repairs with big hours. Mechanics want high ratio of assigned to actual repair hours.

What's the result? Quality work impossible; mechanics cut corners; service writers inflate problems; dealer, in agreement, blames problems on manufacturer.

What about the customer? He or she is running the gauntlet, paying for repairs poorly done, problems caused by shoddy work, even problems that never existed.

The flat-rate pay system is a lose-lose proposition for consumers. On the one hand, if a competent technician truly needs 3.6 hours to perform a repair properly, but the manufacturer has said that it will only pay 1.2 hours for that repair regardless, a dealership that wants to stay in business will tell its technicians to get the repair done in 1.2 hours no matter what. Technicians cannot perform quality repairs if they are not given sufficient time to do so.

On the other hand, if a manufacturer will pay for 1.2 hours for that repair no matter how little time the repair actually takes, it provides a strong incentive for technicians to do the work as quickly as possible—no matter how poorly—so they can move on and get paid for other work. Either way, the consumer's vehicle doesn't always get fixed properly.

How Technicians Are Paid

Most technicians are paid a commission based on what they *flag*. Flagged hours are not real hours worked; they are the manufacturer's set time for each repair done. The technician will make a given wage per flat-rate hour. Few repair shops guarantee a minimum income, so if a technician flags no time in a given day, he makes no money at all. For these technicians, the motivation is to flag as many hours per day as possible.

Because the technician flags a set amount of hours per repair regardless of how little time the repair actually takes, it is not impossible, or even that uncommon, for a technician to flag over sixteen hours in an eight-hour day. In fact, it is not unheard of for a fast, crooked technician to flag over eighty hours in a five-day week while working only a little over eight hours per day.

Where is the incentive to do an honest day's work?

If you work as a technician for an auto dealer, the time you spend making repairs bears little or no relationship to the time for which you are paid. Sometimes you can spend forty hours at the shop, but if you didn't flag enough time, you are paid for only twenty. Other times you can spend forty hours but get paid for as much as a hundred.

There's nothing wrong with incentives unless the reward is achieved by shoddy work.

The dealership effectively makes a portion of what the technician flags, so it, too, is interested in having the technician flag as many hours per day as possible. There is little motivation to be honest, and quite a bit of motivation to rip off the consumers.

The Flat-Rate Pay System and Part-Swapping

> Part-Swapping: A vehicle repair technique employed by inexperienced or incompetent technicians. Because they do not understand the problem, they try replacing various parts until the problem goes away, or until they stop trying to fix it.

The auto repair industry has changed over the years as more complex automobiles have created a new kind of technician. Some of these changes have created smarter, better-trained technicians. However, they have also made the part-swapping approach to problem solving much more widespread.

Part-swapping can sometimes be a legitimate trouble-shooting technique. But what about when the problem is intermittent? What about the cost of all those good parts that needn't have been replaced?

The flat-rate pay system only encourages part-swapping. Poor or inexperienced technicians are not paid for the time it would take them to diagnose and repair a problem properly. One way they can make sure that they don't spend more time than they can flag is to throw a part at the problem, bill for it, and hope the problem goes away.

An unpleasant consequence of part-swapping occurs when the problem shows up a second time. Many manufacturers will refuse to reimburse a dealership for repeated warranty repairs for the same complaint, citing inefficiency on the first attempt. For example, suppose a vehicle's engine runs rough. The technician replaces the spark plugs, but the car comes back with the same complaint. If the dealership wrote it up on the repair order as the same complaint, then the manufacturer would assume correctly that the dealer hadn't done a proper repair the first time. The manufacturer would reject the warranty claim, and the dealership would not be paid for the repair.

To avoid this, it is in the best interest of both the dealership and the technician to find something different to blame so that they can make it look like a different repair and get the manufacturer to pay for it. They certainly aren't going to admit that they made a mistake the first time. Instead, this time the repair order may say that the engine hesitates and surges.[4]

Says one former technician: *"Part of the reason I changed careers was because I was so frustrated by working in such a crooked environment. Bad technicians that lacked morals made the most money and honest ones lagged behind significantly."*

Work Faster, Not Better

A fast technician flags 80 hours of work. His actual time to accomplish the work might be only 38 hours. Dealerships love these high-speed technicians, because they make the company a ton of money. These technicians are the dealer's darlings. They will get bonuses, pats on the back, and "Best Technician of the Month" awards.

Some managers even base their technicians' hourly rate on the number of hours flagged. Technicians flagging over 80 hours per week get a two-dollar-per-hour raise over a 40-hour technician. When honest technicians ask their managers for raises, they are told, *"You want a raise? Flag more hours!"*

Nothing wrong with working fast, but how often have you seen good work proceed from fast work?

---

4. See chapter 7, 85, "Slicing and Dicing" the Defect.

It is a rare exception to find a dealership giving a raise to the technician with the highest customer satisfaction.

After-Warranty Repair Times

The problems with the flat-rate pay system do not end when the warranty expires and the manufacturer no longer dictates the amount of time for each repair. Dealers create and use their own aftermarket flat-rate manuals for after-warranty repairs. These manuals usually multiply the manufacturer's warranty time standards by 1.5. For instance, a technician changing a part might flag 1.1 hours under warranty, but flags 1.7 hours after the warranty has expired.

Vehicle Diagnostics

In most cases, there is not really a flat-rate time for diagnosis. This means that a good technician who can troubleshoot a problem in 0.5 hours may charge significantly less than a clueless technician who spends two days swapping parts to figure it out.

Always ensure the technician makes note of computer tests done on the repair order. It can certainly cause a difference if there is trouble with the vehicle later.

Diagnostic tools in the repair shop seldom find the problem. They only point in the general direction. In fact, during diagnostic tests, a significant percentage of defective electrical and electronic parts typically pass, returning "no fault found" codes even though they are defective. This makes the clueless technician's job take even longer.

An honest, competent technician who can diagnose a problem in 0.5 hours will flag 0.5 hours. A competent but slightly less-than-honest technician may feel that he should not be penalized for being good at his job. He may flag 0.8 hours.

The clueless technician, honest or not, may flag two full days for the diagnosis, plus the cost of any additional parts that he swapped. There is very little incentive for the shop owner to intervene unless the customer complains. And there is very little likelihood of that, because the customer has no idea that the two-day job should have taken only half an hour.

Intermittent Problems

Many electrical and drivability problems on today's automobiles are intermittent. Not all technicians can troubleshoot problems accurately. Of those, only a portion can troubleshoot intermittent and more difficult problems. The technicians may guess and swap parts until the problems are solved or the consumer runs out of money.

If you find a good technician you can trust, stick with him and tell all your friends.

When the Dealership Is in Trouble

A variety of things can put a dealership in financial trouble: it hasn't sold enough vehicles at a profit; its costs are too high; technicians haven't been flagging enough warranty repair time. These problems make management start looking for ways to cut costs.

Where Can They Cut Costs?

When management starts looking at cutting costs, four things are always at the top of the list:

- Cut people

- Cut pay

- Cut quality

- Cut training

These actions do not exist in a vacuum. When you cut any one of them, it affects all of the others. And every one of them hurts the consumer.

Cutting People

Regrettably, this is one of the easiest ways for management to improve the bottom line: cut people, eliminating their salaries. Unfortunately, having fewer competent salespeople and technicians just aggravates the problems that led to the dealer's financial trouble in the first place. It addresses only the immediate symptom—lack of money—instead of solving the underlying reasons why there is no money.

Cutting Pay

Reducing the salaries of the people who do all the work is just another shortsighted way to address the symptom instead of the real problems. People who get paid less do not tend to focus on improving their job performance.

Slashing Quality Budgets

At the heart of any company's lack of success is the lack of quality throughout the organization.[5] The measure of quality is not limited to physical products. It includes every service the organization delivers. Every automobile dealership provides just as much service as products.

When dealerships start cutting quality, everything starts looking frayed around the edges. You find the car you want, but the salesman is rude. You buy a beautiful new car, but it is delivered filthy. You take your car in for an oil change, but must wait three days. All of these things are aspects of quality, and all of them are affected when the organization devotes insufficient resources to delivering quality service.

---

5. See chapter 5, 43, "The Need for Lemon Law."

Slashing Training Budgets

There isn't a dealership in the United States today that doesn't have serious problems finding and keeping competent technicians. Yet training budgets rarely seem adequate to address that need. Cutting training budgets is just another shortsighted approach that, in the end, causes more problems than it solves.

Poorly trained technicians can be as much of a problem as defects in a new vehicle. They can prolong, and even aggravate, any problem that was manufactured into the car originally. Worse, they can cause problems where none previously existed. Vehicle complexity alone makes higher levels of training essential.

Cutting back on training is like treating a headache by shooting yourself in the foot.

Medicine uses the word *iatrogenic* to describe a medical problem caused by the doctor or the treatment. How many of your car's problems were caused by an under-trained technician?

It's stupid and cruel to order a mechanic to do work he or she hasn't been trained to do.

There's a difference between a technician and a mechanic. It's called training.

CHAPTER 7
The Gauntlet

*"It is a tale told by an idiot, full of sound
and fury, signifying nothing."*
—William Shakespeare, *Macbeth*

"If You Can't Fix Their Car, Fix Their Head"

Believe it or not, this is an actual quote from a service manager
at a large automobile dealership.

"It's easy, Joe. If you can't fix their car, fix their
head. Tell him, 'No problem found,' again.
That'll drive them crazy every time."

What does this mean? In simple terms, it means that your automobile, motor home, boat, or motorcycle has defects that the dealer and manufacturer cannot—or do not want to—fix. So instead of fixing them, they will try to convince you that the vehicle doesn't need to be fixed, or that you don't want it fixed.

In other chapters we talk about the driving forces behind what eventually becomes your ordeal of lemon ownership: the corporate big picture. This chapter will lay out many of the actual deceptions and procedures that manufacturers and dealers employ, designed to make you give up and go away.

The Manufacturer Knows About the Problem

As you read about the gauntlet, fix this firmly in your mind: most of the time, the manufacturer and its dealerships know all about the defective condition in the vehicle. In all likelihood, the defect was manufactured into the vehicle through engineering error, poor quality parts, inadequate quality control, deficient manufacturing procedures, or simply the statistics of manufacturing millions of vehicles.[1]

The Gauntlet: What Did I Do to Deserve This?

The lemon gauntlet is not a theory; it is not a metaphor; it is very real.

Long before westerners arrived in the United States, Native Americans were required to run the gauntlet as a test of courage. It wasn't easy. Two parallel lines of warriors were formed, and the warrior to be tested had to run between them. Each warrior in the line had a club. Every warrior took a shot. There was no holding back. Blood was spilled.

---

1. See chapter 5, 52, Complexity and Malfunctions: A Catch-22.

This lemon gauntlet lasts longer and is far more
painful and destructive than the tests of courage
experienced by early Indian warriors.

These days, manufacturers and dealers do the same thing
to consumers. They don't use sticks and clubs. They use
deception, delay, and occasionally fraud.

It was a lot easier for the warrior to run as fast as he
could for a few minutes. He took his lumps and it was
over. Not so with vehicle manufacturers and dealers.
When manufacturers put you through the gauntlet, it
can last months, even years.

Manufacturers and dealerships do not think this is unjust. They think it is business, and good business at that. If you are the owner of a lemon vehicle, you have probably been given a runaround that makes getting a permit from your local bureaucracy seem like taking a vacation to Disneyland.

This runaround is mental and financial torture, and can take many months, even years. The gauntlet consumes incredible amounts of wasted time and costs that you did not anticipate and probably can ill afford. Less visibly, but certainly as important, it can ruin your peace of mind, cause family upsets and arguments, and even endanger your life.

Entering the Gauntlet

The lemon gauntlet begins with the second visit to the dealer to repair the same defect.

The *lemon gauntlet* typically begins when you arrive the second time for a repair of the same defect. The threat of this being a potential lemon sets off alarms at the dealership.

"Uh-oh," they say to themselves. *"If we can't repair it, we'd better employ every trick we know to make this person give up and go away."*

This attitude is incredibly cynical—even cruel—because it undermines the owner's safety and peace of mind. To make someone give up, manufacturers and dealerships have to remove hope. They have to take an owner, who starts out happy and proud of having a new car, and drive them into apathy and despair.

> Think about that for a moment. Remove hope!

This is not an isolated incident of bad corporate behavior. This behavior is pervasive and widespread. There is not one car manufacturer that doesn't employ one or more of the methods described below.

Figure 7.1 shows the seemingly endless methods that dealerships and manufacturers employ to get you to give up and go away.

Remember when that fellow in the movie said, *"I'm mad as hell, and I'm not going to take it anymore"*? This is a much better attitude than, *"I can't do anything. This is going to go on forever. I better just sell this piece of %$@#$&! and get something that works."*

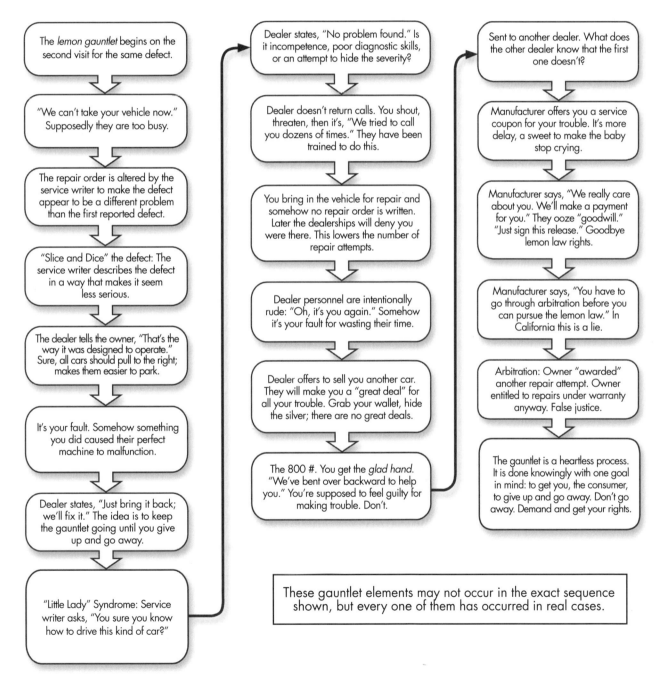

Figure 7.1. A Typical Lemon Gauntlet

Stupid Dealer Tricks

The gauntlet begins at the dealers. Manufacturers train their dealership personnel in ways to help them identify and deal with customers who might be developing potential lemon claims. Of course, the easiest way to prevent a lemon claim would be to fix the vehicle, but sometimes that's just too hard for them.

We Can't Take Your Car Now

When Mr. and Mrs. Jones tried to make an appointment to get their car fixed the first time, and the dealer told them that they were too busy and that it would be two weeks before they could work on the car, this was the opening salvo in what would become Mr. and Mrs. Jones's personal lemon war. Nothing wears the car owner down more surely than the sheer amount of time it takes to get anything done. The dealer and manufacturer know this. They also know that time—wasted time—is on their side.

Repair Order Alteration

One of the tests for determining whether a vehicle is a lemon is whether there have been repeated repairs for the same problem.[2] To avoid this, the dealership will often write up the same problem in different ways to make it look like different problems. This is subtle, and you might not even notice it, so pay attention when the service writer at the dealership fills in your repair order.

For example, you describe the problem as "Check Engine light comes on, car stalls." The service writer suggests it might be something wrong with the Emission Control System, so he writes down "ECS problem."[3] This is not what you said. Be absolutely certain the service writer puts down exactly what you tell him to write down. It matters!

2. See chapter 8, 99, "How Can I Tell If My Car Is a Lemon?"
3. See chapter 1, 3, "A New Car Lemon Story."

"Okay, I have this down as a purge valve replacement, Mr. Jones."

"That's wrong, Mr. Service Writer. I want the repair order to say exactly what I told you: Car stalls repeatedly!"

"Slicing and Dicing" the Defect

This is an extension of the Repair Order Alteration gambit. The problem is *Check Engine light comes on, car stalls*. The dealer will try to make this problem look like something else, something less serious. Here are a few possibilities.

- A short in an electrical harness

- Broken or disconnected vacuum hoses

- Emission Control System problem

- Ignition System fault

If the dealer can write down something different on each repair order, the stalling problem can be made to look like it isn't really the defect. Then the manufacturer can argue that it has successfully repaired four different problems, instead of having repeated failed repair attempts for the same problem.

Slicing and dicing has another benefit for dealers and manufacturers: it often makes your problem sound trivial. Car stalling, intermittent or otherwise, is a serious safety problem. But *"We found an electrical short"* sounds a lot less serious than *"My car stalled while I was driving on the freeway!"*

That's the Way It Was Designed to Operate

The dealer is hoping that the consumer will be gullible enough to believe that the defect isn't really a defect at all. This is just another attempt to fix the consumer's head. Here is an example from an actual case:

Hard as such a story is to believe, there are many of them.

A lady had a car that pulled severely to the right whenever she drove it. It pulled so hard that her arms and shoulders ached just holding the car in a straight line. The dealer told her that this was a designed-in safety feature to ensure that, if she fell asleep while driving, the vehicle would turn into the curb.

This is not something we made up; it actually happened. Truth is often stranger than fiction.

It's Your Fault

The service writer or technician wants the owner to believe that he or she is too stupid to understand how to use a car. Dealerships actually want consumers to believe their cars are fine, and that if they only knew something about cars, there never would have been a problem in the first place.

Just Bring It Back, We'll Fix It

When consumers start calling to complain that repairs have failed, both dealers and manufacturers tell them to return their vehicles for further repairs. They give the appearance of being extraordinarily helpful. In reality, they don't have any more reason to believe they can fix it this time than they had the last three times. It's just more delay, more misdirection. The defect still doesn't get fixed. Nothing has changed, except that you have wasted more time and acquired more stress.

The "Little Lady" Syndrome

Dealers use this particular obnoxious tactic on all consumers, but for some reason it seems directed primarily to women—hence the name "little lady" syndrome. The service manager at the dealer says, *"Honey, are you sure you are using the right kind of gas?"* Or the mechanic says, *"Oh, that's the way this model works, dear."*[4]

When the dealership's people tell you that you don't know how to drive the car, or to have the oil checked regularly, or even how to tighten the gas cap, what they really mean is, "There's nothing wrong with our car; there's something wrong with you." It is patronizing and it is ridiculous.

No Problem Found

This excuse comes up most often when a defect is intermittent; for example, maybe your vehicle stalls only once or twice a month. The problem is real, but the technicians at the dealership might have to do some serious diagnostic work to discover it. As an excuse, it has also been used when the dealer knew exactly what the problem was.

---

4. See chapter 3, 25, "A Used Car Lemon Story."

It is much easier for the technician just to take a five-minute test drive and write "NPF" on the repair order—no problem found. It also makes it appear as though you were just imagining things, and there is really nothing wrong with your car.[5] Maybe the repair order will say "Cannot verify," or "Unable to duplicate." It's all the same thing.

Writing "No problem found" is much easier than spending time trying to diagnose the real problem. It also gives technicians more time to flag simpler repairs for other people, making more money. But this tactic can also help the manufacturer.

Most lemon laws look at whether the manufacturer has had a reasonable number of repair attempts. Manufacturers love to argue that, if the dealer didn't actually do any work on a repair visit—because it couldn't duplicate your problem—then that visit doesn't count as a repair attempt.[6] Remember Mr. and Mrs. Jones—six repair visits, but only three repair attempts according to the manufacturer and the arbitrator?[7]

> Every time you take your vehicle in for repair, whether they do anything or not, is a repair attempt.

Dealer Doesn't Return Calls

There is an army of people at the dealership, yet somehow you can't get anyone to return your calls. When you finally reach the service writer, he tells you that he tried to reach you many times. It wasn't his fault; it must have been your fault. Your answering machine must have lost all of his messages (but no one else's?). And when you finally do get through, the appointment is always next week or longer.

5. See chapter 3, 25, "A Used Car Lemon Story."
6. See chapter 8, 99, "How Can I Tell If My Car Is a Lemon?"
7. See chapter 1, 11, No More Visits: They Try Arbitration.

"Why don't you bring it in next week, Mrs. Jones?
We're too busy...stall....blah...lie..."

What really happened here? After you return complaining more than once, the service writer labels you as trouble and your vehicle as a potential lemon. His refusal to talk to you is just part of the gauntlet—create more delay and more frustration, and hope that you will finally give up and go away. Of course, he can't admit that; so when he finally has to call you back, he pretends the problem is on your end. You know better.

No Repair Order Is Written

If you take your vehicle to the dealer, for any reason, under no circumstances leave without the dealer writing a repair order. Regardless of whether the dealer does anything, get a repair order, even if it states, "We didn't do anything to the vehicle." Be absolutely certain that the service writer puts the exact reason why you brought the vehicle in on the repair order.

In a lemon law case the vehicle owner's paper trail proceeds from information written on repair orders. It is essential that the customer be able to show that they gave the dealer every opportunity to repair the defective vehicle.

Dealer Is Intentionally Rude

The service writer greets your call with, *"Oh, you again!"*[8] His attitude is that you are just an amateur who doesn't understand anything about cars and insists on wasting his valuable time. You are not a valued customer; you have become the enemy. Many consumers are naturally intimidated by people in a position of authority. The service writer hopes to make you feel so humiliated that you will stop complaining about your car's problems.

Dealer Offers to Sell You a New Car

At some point, even the most patient consumer will realize that the dealer simply cannot fix the car. The dealer still doesn't want you to invoke the lemon law, so the sales manager will step in. *"Because you have been such a good customer,"* he will generously offer to take your defective vehicle off your hands and get you into a brand-new vehicle. *"Have I got a deal for you!"*

> A good deal would be if the vehicle you bought ran as advertised!

8. See chapter 3, 28, Used Car: Third Repair Attempt.

The dealer is not doing this out of goodwill, despite what you might be told. You will soon learn that your *used* vehicle isn't worth that much as a trade-in. The new models are more expensive, even with the "goodwill" discount. The bottom line is that you would end up having to pay thousands of dollars for the privilege of giving back your lemon and getting something decent to drive. That's not how the lemon law usually works.

There are no good deals in the gauntlet. If you fall for the dealer's ruse, you are going to lose money. Why should you lose your hard-earned money? All you want is what you paid for in the first place.

Stupid Manufacturer Tricks

If you've made it this far, and successfully navigated through every trick the dealer threw at you, you might think your ordeal would be over. Unfortunately, it's not: you now face the manufacturer who designed the gauntlet to begin with. Good luck.

For a manufacturer to accept a vehicle as a lemon is, on most occasions, a dead loss. The manufacturer isn't going to let this happen without a fight.

The *Glad Hand*

> Glad hand: A warm and hearty, but often insincere, welcome or greeting.

Manufacturers have toll-free customer service numbers or consumer hotlines that you can call. They are usually found in the owner's manual or warranty booklet. By the time you try them, you are probably deep into the gauntlet.

The customer service people are so nice, so helpful. It is such a contrast to the runaround you have been getting from your dealer. They listen. They sympathize with you. They stress how important your satisfaction is to them. They "feel your pain." Most importantly, they tell you that they truly understand.

If the manufacturer really feels your pain, why, after dealing with their representative, do you still feel it?

The purpose of the *glad hand* is to calm you down, and to soften you up for the next stage of the gauntlet. They want to make you more receptive to whatever the manufacturer is going to offer you next, be it more repairs, a visit from a "specialist," or a few hundred dollars in exchange for a waiver of all of your rights.

Try a Different Technician

The customer service hotline often sends you to another dealership. *"We're sorry you're having problems with your regular dealer, Mr. and Mrs. Jones, but your warranty is good at hundreds of locations."*

The manufacturer may also offer to send in a technical specialist to personally diagnose your car and supervise repairs. In either case, the implication is that this new person or this new dealer will really be able to fix your car this time.

Why go to another dealer? What does another dealer know that yours doesn't? Why should you need a specialist? Is your regular dealer incompetent? If so, it isn't your fault; it's their responsibility.

The manufacturer has no answer to your problem. The manufacturer has no reason to think that a new dealership or a technical specialist would have better luck fixing your vehicle. It's just more delay.

We Want to Reward You for Your Patience

If you seem very upset, the manufacturer may offer you something to compensate you for your trouble. This supposed compensation could take many forms:

- A service coupon, good for a free oil change.

- A few hundred dollars toward your next monthly payment, to make up for all the time your vehicle has been in the shop.

- A discount on a brand-new automobile from the same manufacturer. (Ford used to call these "Owner Appreciation Certificates." But don't forget that there are no good deals in the gauntlet!)

- Maybe even a few thousand dollars in cash, if you will only go away.

Guess who has an army of attorneys to deal with irate consumers?

The manufacturer isn't admitting that there is a problem, but is making you this offer purely as a goodwill gesture, to reward you for your patience. But you don't want a reward. You want your car to work. It's appeasement, but it doesn't solve anything. You still have a defective automobile that no one will fix.

Just Sign This Release, Mr. and Mrs. Jones

After offering you one of the "rewards" mentioned above, the manufacturer may ask you to sign a little innocent-looking piece of paper, called a *release*, in exchange for the goodwill gesture.

DO NOT SIGN ANYTHING!

If you sign a release, you are agreeing to give up your rights under the lemon law. This is one of the worst things a manufacturer can try to trick a consumer into doing. Every other part of the gauntlet is designed to delay, to frustrate, to distract, to appease—anything to stop you from bringing a lemon lawsuit. If you persevere, however, you can successfully run the gauntlet.

This nasty bit of trickery, in contrast, utterly forecloses any hope you might have of getting a replacement or refund for your lemon. You will no longer have any legal rights. The gauntlet is over, and you didn't make it.

Don't Get Help

At some point in the gauntlet, you may get so frustrated that you start asking the dealer or manufacturer about your rights under the lemon law. Invariably, you will be told that you should not even think of filing a lawsuit while they are *"bending over backwards to help you."* They will reassure you that the lemon law doesn't offer you anything more than what they are offering you.

The manufacturer and dealer will tell you that, no matter what, you absolutely should not involve an attorney. They will tell you an attorney will just cost you more money, and that, once lawyers are involved, the manufacturer won't be able to *help* you anymore. Hogwash!

They will tell you anything they can to discourage you from consulting a professional. They know that you are nearing the end of the gauntlet. If you were to get legal advice, you would learn that they have been intentionally misleading you. You would learn your rights, and you could choose to pursue those rights.

Informal Dispute Resolution: Arbitration

Some lemon laws may require you to go through an informal arbitration process before you can file a lemon lawsuit. Others may not. However, if you call the customer hotline from one of those states, they may still tell you that you have to go through arbitration before you can seek any other remedy.

Arbitration is rarely helpful, even if you win. For example, the arbitrator may issue an eloquently worded opinion finding that your defect exists, but that "in all fairness" it looks as if it could be repaired. So, instead of awarding you the refund or replacement that the law requires, you are "awarded" just another repair attempt. But you were already entitled to further repairs under your warranty. The arbitration award gives you nothing you didn't already have.

Worse yet, the arbitrator may decide that the manufacturer must repair only one of your vehicle's minor problems, rather than your major concern. For example, Mr. and Mrs. Jones's vehicle repeatedly stalled in traffic, but the arbitrator ordered the manufacturer to fix only their air conditioning. They wasted months on arbitration, and they were left right where they started, with a vehicle that repeatedly stalled in traffic.

Gauntlet Summary

The gauntlet is not an accident of fate. It is a deliberate policy. It begins with top management at the manufacturer. It's not personal: the manufacturers do not know who you are, or care. They just want those irritating consumers to give up and go away.

For every consumer who does not give up, there are probably ten who do. Don't be one of those ten.

I urge you not to give up. Remember what I have told you here. Call your attorney, regardless of whether you are told it won't do any good. Remember, if you go away, they don't pay.

PART 3

The Lemon Law and You

CHAPTER 8

How Can I Tell If My Vehicle Is a Lemon?

> *"Historically we've said, 'Quality costs money,'*
> *while our competition overseas has been saying,*
> *'Quality makes money.' And they've been proving it."*
> —Harrington

What Is a Lemon?

The term *lemon* is not defined in California's lemon law, the federal Magnuson-Moss Act, or in any other state's lemon law. It is slang, pure and simple. It has taken on the meaning of a *bad vehicle* or product that makes you feel bitter because it is so substandard in performance and cannot be fixed.

The term originally derives from gambling. On the old slot machines, the lemon symbol had no match. Thus, if a lemon appeared, there could be no possible winning combination and the player was guaranteed to lose. Without lemon laws, consumers stuck with defective vehicles were also guaranteed to lose.

The laws of the various states define a vehicle that qualifies for a refund or return, which we refer to as a *lemon*. Most define a lemon as a vehicle that the manufacturer has not successfully repaired after a certain number of attempts, or after the vehicle has been out of service for a particular number of days.

> Throughout this book, I use the term *manufacturer*, because the warranty typically comes from the manufacturer. However, the same principles apply to anyone else, such as a distributor or dealership, who gives a written warranty at the time of sale.

Which Vehicles Qualify?

Many state lemon laws limit their application to motor vehicles. Motorcycles, motor homes, mopeds, and other similar products are often excluded. Not all states are so limited, however. Consult the appendix for details on your particular state's lemon law.

We have represented clients with automobiles, boats, motor homes, and motorcycles.

For example, while California's lemon law contains several special provisions that apply only to motor vehicles, it generally covers all *consumer goods*. The federal Magnuson-Moss Act similarly applies to any consumer product, not just motor vehicles. Laws like this cover not only motorcycles and motor homes but also boats, snowmobiles, skateboards, and even personal computers, toasters, and blenders.

What About Used Vehicles?

Most state lemon laws apply only to new products; however, there are exceptions. Many lemon laws apply to anyone who is entitled to the benefits of the written warranty, regardless of whether he or she was the original purchaser. California's lemon law generally applies to any used goods, so long as they come with a written warranty. Federal law requires used car dealers to provide a Buyer's Guide, which among other things must either set forth any applicable warranty or state that the vehicle is being sold "as is."

What About Leases?

Many state lemon laws, including California's, cover vehicles that are leased as well as those that are purchased. Some lemon laws do not. Others cover leases only of a certain minimum length. Consult the law of your particular state to determine its coverage.[1]

---

1. See appendix A, Lemon Law Summary All Fifty States.

What About Business Use?

Lemon laws also limit their application to vehicles purchased or leased for personal use, but not all do. The Magnuson-Moss Act, for example, applies to all products that are *normally* used for personal use. If you use your pickup truck primarily for your business, the federal lemon law should still cover it if it is the kind of truck that is normally used for personal, family, or household purposes.

Remember, if you have a truck, the weight of the vehicle may be significant. Check the lemon laws for your state.

California's lemon law was recently amended to expand its protection to cover vehicles owned by individuals or small businesses, even if used primarily for business purposes. As I have mentioned, California has one of the country's strongest lemon laws. If you live in another state and you wish your lemon law had greater protection, write your legislators!

What Is a Defect?

A defect is something the vehicle does (for example, pulls to the left) or does not do (for example, won't start) that falls below the standard set forth in the warranty. Some states, like California, use the term *nonconformity* in their lemon laws. A nonconformity is essentially the same as a defect.

Some states use the word *condition* in their lemon laws. If a vehicle continues to have the same condition after a number of repair attempts, then it doesn't matter what specific *defect* was causing it. This prevents manufacturers and dealers from arguing that they have not had enough attempts to repair any individual defect because the parts replaced or repairs performed were different on each repair visit.

What Is Substantial Impairment?

Impair: to cause to diminish, as in strength, value, or quality. To damage or make worse by or as if by diminishing.

Most lemon laws also limit the definition of a lemon to a vehicle in which the defective condition substantially impairs its use, value, or safety. In many states, whether impairment is substantial is determined from the point of view of the consumer, not the manufacturer. This suggests a subjective standard, from the point of view of the particular consumer in each case. However, there is a wide variation of interpretation from state to state.

Certainly defects that prevent the vehicle from starting, stopping, turning, or otherwise operating properly should be substantial impairment. Defects in important components, like the air conditioning system, or even significant paint defects that require repainting the entire vehicle might be substantial impairment. Whether a defect is a substantial impairment is ultimately a decision for a judge or jury.

How the consumer feels about his or her experiences with the vehicle may assist a jury in determining whether the vehicle is a lemon. If you have a new vehicle that doesn't work as promised, it can certainly leave a bitter taste in your mouth.

Defects in the following areas often constitute substantial impairment, depending on the nature of the defect:

- Engine

- Transmission

- Brakes

- Powertrain items

- Fuel system

- Emission Control System

- Seat belts

Substantial defects are definitely not limited to those listed above. These are just examples. A malfunctioning radio could be substantial impairment if it turned out to be just one symptom of a more pervasive problem affecting the vehicle's entire electrical system.

Impaired Use

One buys an automobile for pleasure and utility. Getting to work, taking the children to school, or going on a weekend drive are all legitimate uses for an automobile. Anything that makes it more difficult for a consumer to use a vehicle in the way that he or she intended impairs the vehicle's use.

A potato peeler ought to, at the very least, peel potatoes. If it does not, its use is impaired.

Impaired use does not mean *no use*. Manufacturers love to argue that, so long as the consumer is still driving the vehicle at all, there has been no substantial impairment in use. This argument is wrong because lemon laws are not limited to problems that prevent use altogether. The argument makes as little sense as arguing that a defect does not *impair safety* unless the driver actually dies in a car crash.

For example, suppose a consumer purchases a vehicle with the specific intent to use it at least twice per year to visit her mother who lives in another state. The vehicle has defects that make her uncomfortable driving it on long trips, so she never uses it to visit her mother. Her use of the vehicle has been impaired even if she still drives it to work every day.

As another example, suppose a vehicle is in the shop for repairs for 120 days during the first year of ownership. This clearly impairs the owner's use of the vehicle, even if he can use it for any purpose when it is not in the shop.

A defect can impair a vehicle's use even if it does not directly affect the amount the vehicle is driven. For example, if the air conditioning emits a stench so pervasive that it gags the driver or triggers an asthma attack in a family member, it is not fit for its intended use.

Impaired Value

Value is not limited to strictly monetary value.

Impaired value is probably the most common ground for invoking a lemon law. In fact under the old Commercial Code, it is the only ground.[2] In most states, value is not limited to strictly monetary value; it includes every aspect of the intangible concept of what a vehicle is worth to its owner.

One definition of value suggests that there should be an adequate return on investment. At the very least, the owner has the right to expect the full use and enjoyment of a new car. Consider the following examples:

- The transmission in a brand-new car fails the day after purchase. When the consumer returns the vehicle to the dealership, the dealer puts in a new transmission from some other vehicle—not the same year, maybe not even the same model. Although the replaced transmission may not have had a substantial effect on the vehicle's market value, the consumer has lost confidence in the integrity of his brand-new car. His faith is shaken: the vehicle's value is substantially impaired to him.

- A consumer buys a brand-new car for $40,000. Shortly after purchase it develops an intermittent problem in which the Check Engine light goes on, the engine whines, and the entire vehicle shudders. She takes it back to the dealership six times, and every single time she is told they can find nothing wrong. It may turn out that the problem could be easily fixed with the replacement of a two-dollar piece of plastic. It does not matter. The vehicle makes her miserable, and its value to her is substantially impaired.

2. See chapter 4, 35, "A Brief History of Lemon Law."

- A college student buys her first brand-new vehicle with her own money. Imagine the sense of accomplishment, the pride of ownership, the feelings of happiness, she anticipates. Now imagine what she feels instead when the vehicle rattles like an old jalopy and belches thick black smoke wherever she goes, making her the laughingstock of her neighbors and classmates. It does not matter how cheaply the problem could be fixed, or how much money she could get if she had it appraised. The vehicle has lost its value to her.

Obviously, these are not all the possible examples of substantially impaired value. They simply illustrate that *substantial impairment in value* often does not depend on dollar figures. Value, like beauty, is in the eye of the beholder. When consumers experience the frustration of repeated failed repair visits, they do not get the value they paid for: the experience that should have accompanied buying a new vehicle.

Impaired Safety

Common sense suggests that if your vehicle is unsafe and you have made the vehicle available to the dealer for repairs, you ought to be able to give it back and get either a replacement or a refund. Examples of safety issues include

- brake failure

- vehicle stalling while driving

- broken seat belts

- unresponsive steering

- intermittently defective headlights.

Unfortunately, all too often manufacturers seem to view their customers as human guinea pigs, and refuse to take responsibility for potential safety hazards, no matter how serious, until there has been an accident. Again, lemon laws cover defects that impair safety, not just defects that make vehicles completely unsafe.

Under many lemon laws, safety is not a simplistic or narrow concept, limited to conditions that could cause an accident. A vehicle might not be unsafe if its antilock braking system doesn't work, but it is certainly less safe. A faulty gas gauge, perhaps minor in itself, could leave a driver stranded in an unfamiliar area in the middle of the night. Anything that makes a driver or passenger feel less secure can be a substantial impairment in safety.

Reasonable Opportunity to Repair

This is one of those areas where a caution about the importance of reading the warranty is essential.

A vehicle with a defect, even a substantial defect, is not automatically a lemon. Usually the manufacturer is entitled to a reasonable opportunity to repair the vehicle. The vehicle is a lemon only if the manufacturer fails to repair it.

Repeated Repairs for the Same Problem

Many states, California included, presume that four repair attempts for the same defect is enough. Some states—again, including California—allow relief under the lemon law after fewer repair attempts, if the defect is a serious safety risk. Before these laws existed, it was not uncommon for manufacturers to insist that they be allowed yet another chance to repair even after twenty or thirty failed attempts.

Manufacturers will often argue that a repair visit should count as a repair attempt only if their dealership actually performed some kind of repair. If a dealership claims that it cannot duplicate a problem, or that the condition is normal, then it does no work on the vehicle. Even if you bring your vehicle in for repairs eight times for the same problem, if the dealership tried to fix it only once or twice, then the manufacturer will argue that it had only one or two repair attempts.[3]

The manufacturer's argument doesn't hold water. Your only duty is to give the manufacturer an opportunity to repair, by bringing your car back to an authorized dealer. It is not your fault if the dealer does not take advantage of the opportunity. All of your repair visits count, regardless of what the dealer does or does not do.

> This is one of the reasons it is important to keep all of your repair orders. Repair orders document every time you presented your vehicle for repair. This is your evidence.

Days Out of Service

Most lemon laws also come into play if the vehicle has been in for repairs for a certain number of days. A cumulative total of thirty or more days in the shop is often considered a reasonable opportunity to repair the vehicle, but each state's law is different.

Under this days-out-of-service test, it does not matter whether the repairs are for the same defect or for several different defects. The lemon law gives the manufacturer a reasonable opportunity to repair the vehicle itself, not to repair each individual problem that arises. Thus, a consumer can have a valid lemon law claim when successive defects demand continuous repair, even if the dealership successfully repairs each defect, so long as new problems continue to arise.

---

3. See chapter 1, 3, "A New Car Lemon Story."

Here's a little piece of advice: Once your vehicle has been in for repair the legal number of times, don't take it back if you are pursuing a lemon law case. If they fix it, whether permanently or not, you won't be able to prove the vehicle is defective.

The number of repair attempts is also not significant under the days-out-of-service test. A vehicle that was in the shop for one repair attempt that lasted forty-two days would satisfy this test, as would a vehicle that was in the shop for thirty-five one-day repairs for thirty-five different problems.

The *Shaken Faith* Doctrine

In addition to the question of substantial impairment, the severity of the defect can impact the question of how many repair attempts are reasonable. If a defect indicates that the particular item is of poor quality overall, or is so substantial that the dealer probably could not correct it to the satisfaction of a reasonable buyer, then the buyer need not permit further repair attempts.

Under the old Commercial Code, the seller is entitled to a reasonable opportunity to cure the defect before a buyer can revoke acceptance. However, when the buyer's faith in the goods is so shaken that remedying the specific part or problem would not satisfy a reasonable buyer, the buyer may revoke acceptance and get a refund without allowing any repair. Courts often call this the *shaken faith* doctrine.

Where a consumer has reasonably lost confidence in the performance of a vehicle, the shaken faith doctrine should allow the consumer to say, *"Enough is enough,"* and demand a replacement or refund under the lemon law without allowing any further repair attempts.

More on Accurate Repair Orders

On more than one occasion a client has told me that they don't have all the repair orders, and that the dealership is refusing to provide them. This usually happens after the consumer has begun a lemon law case against the manufacturer. I talked earlier about the need for accurate repair orders. The consumer needs to document the day the vehicle went into the shop for repair and the date the vehicle was delivered to the consumer after the repair. It is from these dates that the consumer is able to prove how many days the vehicle was in the shop for all the various repairs. As noted in the previous section, the number of days in the shop is significant.

The law requires that the dealership provide the vehicle owner all of the repair orders.

If the dealership refuses to provide you with accurate, legible repair orders, you may instruct them in the law.

> Make sure that your repair orders reflect accurately the day your vehicle went in the shop and when it came out. If the repair order is not accurate, do not sign it.

A common misconception, often fostered by manufacturers and their dealerships, is that you must return your vehicle to the place you bought it for repairs.[4] This is almost never true. All authorized dealerships act on behalf of the manufacturer, so any authorized dealership can usually perform warranty work on your vehicle. Your warranty booklet should confirm this.

On the other hand, this does not mean that you can take your vehicle anywhere you want. Independent repair shops are often less expensive than authorized dealerships, and you may have a favorite mechanic whom you trust to do a good job on any vehicle. However, if the manufacturer has not specifically authorized the facility to perform service and repairs on its vehicles, taking your vehicle there may be unwise.

---

4. See chapter 1, 10, Fifth Visit: More Runaround with a Lie.

There are at least two ways in which taking your vehicle to an independent repair facility can cause trouble. First, the lemon law allows the manufacturer a reasonable opportunity to repair the vehicle. An independent shop is not acting on behalf of the manufacturer, so any repairs done at such a shop do not qualify as attempts by the manufacturer to repair the vehicle.

Second, manufacturers frequently claim that the work done at an independent shop is the real cause of your vehicle's problems. They may even argue that the independent work voided that portion of the manufacturer's warranty on your vehicle. You should always take your vehicle to an authorized dealer for warranty repair work.

The Lemon Law Presumption

Every lemon law gives the manufacturer a reasonable opportunity to repair the defective vehicle before it is considered a lemon. Most lemon laws also define standards for what they consider a *reasonable* opportunity to repair, based on the number of repair attempts or the total number of days out of service for repairs, within a certain amount of time or mileage.

Once a vehicle has met one of these standards, the law may *presume* that the manufacturer had a reasonable opportunity to repair it. This presumption is one of the most easily misunderstood aspects of the lemon law, so it deserves a closer look.

The Burden of Proof

Normally, people who bring civil lawsuits that go to trial—called plaintiffs—have the burden of proof. This means that they must prove that they have been wronged. Plaintiffs must present their case first. Their burden of proof is to present sufficient evidence that, if believed, would allow a jury to decide in their favor.

If a plaintiff does not satisfy the burden of proof, then the case may never get to the jury. As a somewhat silly example, suppose you have evidence of ten repair attempts for a failed engine. It might sound like you have a good lemon law case, but if the repairs were for some other vehicle that you don't own, the judge would dismiss the case, because no reasonable juror could find that you had met your burden of proof.

The burden of proof can also assist the jury when it is making its decision. Sometimes, the evidence on a disputed issue may be precisely balanced, so that it is just as likely to be true as it is to not be true. If the jury simply cannot decide whom to believe, then the party with the burden of proof on that issue has not satisfied it, and should lose.

What Is a Presumption?

Sometimes the law gives parties in a lawsuit a special way to meet their burden of proving something that they need to prove at trial. If a party proves certain facts, then the jury can presume that some conclusion follows naturally from those facts. The party has not proven the conclusion directly, but the law of the state assumes that it is true, based on the facts that the party has proven.

For example, if you prove that you used the United States Postal Service to mail something to your favorite niece, properly addressed and with proper postage, it leads to the presumption that she actually received it. You don't have any direct proof that she received it—you weren't at her house when the mail arrived—but you have proven all that you need to prove.

Party: a person or group involved in an enterprise; a participant or an accessory; or a group involved in a legal proceeding.

Many presumptions are *rebuttable*. This means that the other party may present evidence to try to rebut, or disprove, the conclusion that the law would ordinarily draw. For example, your niece might testify under oath that she never received whatever you were trying to send her. If an opposing party tries to rebut a presumption, the burden of proof shifts to that party to disprove the natural conclusion. Ultimately, it is still up to the jury to determine whom to believe.

What Is the Lemon Law Presumption?

How does this apply to a lemon law case? As discussed above, a consumer in a lemon law case must prove that the manufacturer had a reasonable number of attempts to repair the vehicle. Consumers often have several ways to establish the *presumption* that the manufacturer had a reasonable number of repair attempts. In California, for example, the presumption is established if any of the following occurs within the first 18 months or 18,000 miles:

- The same defect is subject to repair four or more times.

- The same defect is subject to repair two or more times, and is a serious safety defect that is likely to cause death or bodily injury.

- The vehicle is out of service for repairs for a cumulative total of more than thirty days, for any combination of defects.

If a California consumer proves that a vehicle has been subject to repair four times for the same problem within 18 months or 18,000 miles, then the consumer has met his or her burden of proving that the manufacturer had a reasonable number of repair attempts.

> The presumption helps consumers meet their burden of proof if they have to go to trial.

The Lemon Period

As discussed earlier, state lemon laws generally look at repeated repairs for the same defect or total days in the shop when defining the lemon law presumption. However, most lemon laws also place a time and mileage limit on their presumption; that is, they define the period during which the repair visits must occur in order for the presumption to apply. Some states call this limit a lemon period.

This lemon period varies from state to state. Today's warranty periods are getting longer; there are a few now that are out to 10 years or 100,000 miles. The lemon period is usually not the same as the warranty period—unless, of course, a particular state's lemon law defines it that way.

California recently expanded its lemon period from 12 months or 12,000 miles (whichever comes first) to 18 months or 18,000 miles (whichever comes first). Some states may look only at repair attempts during the first year. Others may look at the first two years or the period of the written warranty, whichever comes first.

Despite its name, the lemon period usually does not define whether the vehicle is a lemon. It defines only whether the consumer can invoke the presumption. More on this below.

Effect of the Lemon Law Presumption

In most states, if the consumer's vehicle meets the presumption during the lemon period, the burden of proof shifts from the consumer to the manufacturer. The manufacturer now has the burden of proving that it did *not* have a reasonable number of repair attempts.

As an example, remember the new car lemon story? Because Mr. and Mrs. Jones's vehicle was in the shop four or more times for the Check Engine light and stalling problem within the first 18 months or 18,000 miles,[5] in California it is presumed that the manufacturer had a reasonable number of repair attempts. If the manufacturer claims that Mr. and Mrs. Jones did not give it enough repair attempts, the burden will be on the manufacturer to prove it.

However, the lemon law presumption is not always available at trial, even if the vehicle would otherwise qualify. Some states place restrictions on a consumer's right to use the presumption. For example, the consumer may have to give a specific written notice to the manufacturer, or may have to go through the manufacturer's informal dispute resolution mechanism. As always, consult the law of your particular state.

What *Isn't* the Lemon Law Presumption?

Many people mistakenly believe that the lemon law presumption establishes the only test for whether a consumer qualifies for a replacement or refund. This simply is not so. In almost every state, including California, the repeated-repairs test and days-in-the-shop test are only guidelines, to help determine whether the manufacturer had a reasonable number of repair attempts.

---

5. See chapter 1, 3, "A New Car Lemon Story."

This is important: In many states, a vehicle can still be a lemon even if no repairs occurred during the lemon period. The decisive test is whether the manufacturer had a reasonable number of attempts to repair the vehicle. Ultimately, the judge or jury in each case still must decide this issue.

> For example, in a case my office recently handled, the manufacturer had sixteen attempts to repair the vehicle, but only three of them were during the lemon period—not enough to qualify for the presumption. The jury properly found that the manufacturer had a reasonable number of repair attempts. When the manufacturer appealed, it lost.

On the other hand, even where a consumer's vehicle qualifies for the presumption it does not mean that the consumer automatically wins. A presumption can help a party in a lawsuit satisfy the burden of proof at trial. In the right circumstances, however, the other party can still overcome the presumption.

In a lemon law case, the manufacturer can usually try to rebut the presumption by proving that it should have had another repair attempt for some reason. If the manufacturer were to offer a good reason why it should have had another opportunity to repair, or if the defect were not substantial, even a vehicle that passes the presumption tests might not be a lemon.

More importantly, the presumption affects only the issue of a reasonable number of repair attempts. It does not affect other things, such as whether the defects substantially impair the vehicle's use, value, or safety to the consumer.

The presumption is not a magic pill that guarantees you automatic victory. Still, if your vehicle qualifies for the presumption, the manufacturer knows that your vehicle has met one of the guidelines in the lemon law.

Don't sleep on your rights.

CHAPTER 9

Warranty and the Broken Promise

> *"A lie is a breach of promise: for whoever seriously addresses his discourse to another, tacitly promises to speak the truth, because he knows that the truth is expected."*
> —William Paley, 1743–1805

Warranty Overview

At the heart of every lemon law is the manufacturer's breach of warranty. It is this broken promise that gives consumers the right to receive a replacement or refund if a vehicle is a lemon.

A manufacturer's warranty is what makes the manufacturer legally responsible for repairs to the consumer's vehicle. It is a form of guarantee. When a manufacturer produces a vehicle, the manufacturer instills confidence in prospective buyers by guaranteeing the vehicle's proper operation for a given period of time or mileage.

The written warranty has also been used as an effective tool to promote sales. Lee Iaccoca, former chairman of the board for Chrysler Corporation, was famous for his seven-year/70,000-mile powertrain warranty. Nowadays, some manufacturers offer warranties lasting as long as ten years or 100,000 miles.

Breach: a violation in the performance of or a failure to perform an obligation created by a promise, duty, or law, without excuse or justification.

Manufacturers are the first to admit, quite candidly, that they offer longer written warranties as an advertising strategy, to improve their sales. Clearly, some accountant determined that the increase in sales revenue offsets the increased costs associated with additional warranty repairs and lemon lawsuits.

Express Warranties

An *express* warranty is typically a written warranty. A new motor vehicle normally comes with several different kinds of written warranties, such as

- bumper-to-bumper warranty

- powertrain warranty

- safety restraint system warranty

- state and federal emissions warranties

- sheet metal and corrosion warranty.

Recreational vehicles often come with many different written warranties, such as

- coach warranty

- chassis warranty

- engine warranty

- transmission warranty.[1]

You may have noticed that your car came with something called a *limited* warranty. Did you ever wonder why? When Congress enacted the federal Magnuson-Moss Act, it defined two types of warranties, *full* and *limited*.[2] A *full* warranty imposes many requirements on the manufacturer—including a requirement that, if a product is defective after a reasonable opportunity to repair it, the manufacturer must replace it or refund the consumer's money. Anything else is a *limited* warranty.

1. See chapter 2, 15, "A Motor Home Lemon Story."
2. See chapter 4, 35, "A Brief History of Lemon Law."

If a warranty is not specifically labeled as a *limited* warranty, Magnuson-Moss treats it as a full warranty. Congress hoped that consumers would buy only products that came with full warranties, so that the power of the marketplace would force manufacturers to give full warranties. Instead, just about every manufacturer gives a limited warranty, so consumers have no real choice. So much for the power of the marketplace!

How Long Does the Warranty Last?

All written warranties contain a specific time or mileage limit, such as three years or 36,000 miles. However, a warranty does not necessarily expire when the vehicle reaches that limit.

In most states, including California, a manufacturer's duty to repair a defect under warranty can continue beyond the warranty period. When a defect appears during the warranty but repair attempts fail to correct the defect, the warranty period is extended until the defect has actually been fixed. Some states require the consumer to notify the manufacturer that the defect has not been fixed in order to qualify for this extension.

The warranty period is essentially a "discovery" period. The warranty continues to cover any defect discovered during the warranty period, even if the repairs must extend beyond it. This rule was established to prevent manufacturers from performing *Band-Aid* repairs, designed to correct—or hide—the defect only until the warranty expires, and then saying, *"We have no further obligation."* The law requires a permanent cure.

The implied warranty speaks to the ethics of a fair trade. Again, one has the expectation of getting a product that is what its purpose suggests.

Some state lemon laws extend warranties in other ways. For example, California's Song-Beverly Act extends the written warranty by the number of days the vehicle was unavailable to the consumer because it was in the shop for warranty repairs. If a vehicle were in the shop for a total of forty-five days during the warranty period, the warranty would be extended forty-five days from its original date of expiration.

Implied Warranties

An *implied* warranty, unlike an express warranty, is not written down anywhere by the manufacturer. The law imposes these obligations on the manufacturer, the seller, or both as a matter of public policy.

In a few states—including California—the lemon law may create its own implied warranties. In other states, the old Commercial Code implied warranties apply.

Implied Warranty of Merchantability

The word *merchantability* means fitness for ordinary use. When consumers buy a product, they have certain expectations of what the product will do—that it will perform all of the functions that such products normally perform. If a product meets those expectations, then it *fits* the purchaser's needs.

The general test for merchantability requires that the goods be reasonably suitable for the ordinary uses they were manufactured to meet. In fact, one of the definitions of a quality product is its fitness for intended use.[3]

---

3. See chapter 11, 144, Driver Abuse.

As it applies to motor vehicles, the implied warranty of merchantability is a guarantee that they will operate in a safe condition and be substantially free of defects. Every buyer has the right to assume that a new car, with the exception of minor adjustments, will be mechanically new and factory furnished, operate perfectly, and be free of substantial defects.

For example, a motor home ought to allow its owners to drive around the country in comfort, visit Yellowstone Park, sit beneath the awning, and watch the sunset over the Pacific. It should not start only every other day. It should not smell like an open sewer. The extendable room should not slide out on its own while driving in traffic. If it does not operate in a way consistent with its intended use, it is not merchantable.

The implied warranty of merchantability also means that the product is what it says it is. For example, suppose you purchase a vehicle that is supposed to come with an eight-cylinder engine—and even has a V8 emblem on it—but it turns out to have a six-cylinder engine instead. Even though the vehicle may operate perfectly—and thus be fit for its intended use—it still is not merchantable, because it does not have the V8 engine it is supposed to have.

The Privity Trap

Under some state lemon laws—including California's Song-Beverly Act—the manufacturer and the seller give an implied warranty of merchantability. But beware! In other states, the manufacturer does not give any implied warranty, because it has no direct contract with the consumer. This archaic concept is called *vertical privity of contract*.

Privity is a legal term meaning simply that some legal relationship exists between two parties. *Privity of contract* means that the relationship is contractual. When a consumer buys a vehicle from a dealership, there is a sales contract between them. Thus, there is privity of contract, so the dealer gives an implied warranty of merchantability.

There is no sales contract between the consumer and the manufacturer; however, some states consider the manufacturer's written warranty to the consumer to satisfy the contractual-relationship requirement. Other states, like California, have simply abolished the privity requirement outright. In those states that still require privity of contract—and look only for a sales contract, not a written warranty—consumers have reduced rights against manufacturers.

Implied Warranty of Fitness for a Particular Purpose

The implied warranty of merchantability speaks only to the ordinary use of a product. However, another kind of implied warranty applies if the buyer tells the salesperson that he or she intends to use the product for a particular purpose, and the salesperson states that a specific product would be appropriate for that purpose.

It's a nice planter, but can you drive it?

As its name suggests, the implied warranty of fitness for a particular purpose is a promise that the product the seller recommended will, in fact, do what the buyer wanted it to do. The buyer relies on the salesperson's superior knowledge and skill to select a suitable product. Thus, the implied warranty guarantees that the product will be fit for that particular purpose.

While it's all right to rely on the salesperson's knowledge, it would be wise to remember that the seller wants to sell, which sometimes overrides the consumer's needs.

For example, a family looking to purchase a Sport Utility Vehicle may tell the dealership that they want one powerful enough to tow their 10,000-pound boat to the lake. If the dealer recommends a vehicle that cannot handle the boat without overheating, then the vehicle is not fit for the particular purpose the buyers had in mind—even if it otherwise performs just like any other SUV.

Service Contracts

It has become fairly common for dealerships to offer service contracts to buyers of new and used vehicles. Some lemon laws cover breaches of service contracts as well as breaches of warranties, though the remedies may be different.

A great deal of confusion concerning service contracts can arise at the time of sale. Many salespersons refer to a service contract as an *extended warranty*, when it may be something quite different—particularly when considering rights under the lemon law. I will attempt to clear up some of these misunderstandings.

What Is a Service Contract?

A service contract is optional repair coverage, under which someone besides the consumer pays for repairs if something goes wrong. It is typically sold with a new or used vehicle for an additional cost, most often at the time of sale. Sometimes a service contract may be available for purchase even after the sale, if the original written warranty has not yet expired.

There Are Several Types of Service Contracts

- The selling dealer can sell its own service contract, under which that dealer is obligated to perform any covered repairs at its own expense.

- The dealer can sell a service contract on behalf of the original manufacturer, under which the dealer performs covered repairs and the manufacturer reimburses the dealer for its work.

- The dealer can sell a service contract on behalf of an independent company, often called the *contract administrator,* which will decide what to cover and what repairs to authorize in any given situation.

The key differences are who performs the repairs and who pays for the repairs. When your car needs to be repaired or serviced, you may be able to choose among several facilities, or you may be required to return the vehicle to your selling dealer.

Service contracts that make the consumer return to an authorized dealership, sometimes called *captive* service contracts, are favorites of many manufacturers and dealers. The dealership makes a profit from the original sale of the service contract, of course. The contract then brings the consumer back to the dealership for future repairs, and often even for maintenance items that the service contract does not cover. Getting customers to return to the shop means more profit.

Once a manufacturer's original warranty expires, the average consumer will usually go to an independent shop for repairs and service, because prices are so much higher at an authorized dealership. Captive service contracts keep consumers coming back to authorized dealerships, even after the original warranty expires. Dealers have considerable incentive to convince consumers to buy these service contracts with their vehicles.

Service Contract Coverage

A service contract generally covers only things not covered under the original written warranty. It may be available at the same time written warranty coverage is in effect, but more often it comes into effect only after the original warranty expires. Most service contracts have language that specifically excludes anything still covered under the original warranty.

Like the original warranty, a service contract will cover a vehicle for a certain period of time or mileage. Usually, this does not exceed 100,000 miles. For example, a service contract might go into effect upon expiration of the manufacturer's bumper-to-bumper warranty of three years or 36,000 miles, and continue until five years or 75,000 miles, whichever comes first.

Many service contracts provide less coverage than an original warranty. For example, they may not cover the full cost of repair, requiring the consumer to pay a deductible. They may also cover only major vehicle components, like the engine and the transmission, rather than the entire vehicle.

Few service contracts cover all repairs; quite often, common repairs for parts like brakes and clutches are not included. Under a typical bumper-to-bumper warranty, every component is usually covered unless it is specifically excluded. Under a typical service contract, however, a component is covered only if it is specifically listed in the contract.

Many service contract administrators authorize the use of *reconditioned* or *like new* parts instead of actual new parts, even for major repairs. Some consumers are disappointed when they find out that the shop is replacing their defective engine with a reconditioned engine instead of an engine from the factory.

On the other hand, many service contracts offer rental car coverage when the vehicle is in for repairs. As you can see, the terms of any particular service contract can vary dramatically. If you have any questions about a service contract's coverage, make sure to ask them before you agree to buy anything.

The consumer is usually required to follow all of the manufacturer's recommendations for routine maintenance, such as oil and spark plug changes. Failure to do so may void the service contract. Keep detailed records, including receipts.

Service Contracts and Warranties

From a consumer's viewpoint, a service contract and a warranty are functionally the same: both promise that the consumer will not have to pay for repairs in the event of a failure. However, warranties and service contracts may be treated very differently in a lemon law setting.

One notable difference between the two is that a warranty, in addition to promising to perform needed repairs, actually promises that the vehicle has a certain level of quality—that is, that it is free from defects. A service contract generally offers no promise of quality at all, but simply promises some sort of compensation if something does go wrong. It is like an insurance policy.

Many lemon laws distinguish between warranties and service contracts, and they may not give consumers with service contracts the same rights as consumers with warranties. After a reasonable number of failed attempts to repair a vehicle under warranty, you should have the right to a refund or replacement. However, you could theoretically have over one hundred failed attempts to repair the same major defect under a service contract, yet still have no right to a refund or replacement.

Most Common Problem

In my experience, the most frequent problem that consumers come across when trying to get someone else to pay for repairs under a service contract is a dispute over whether the defect is covered. Service contracts, like manufacturers' warranties, typically exclude defects resulting from abuse or lack of maintenance.[4] When a major vehicle component fails, the issue of whether the consumer may have abused or misused the vehicle usually arises. For example, anyone driving a vehicle without proper coolant, or with the oil level dangerously low, runs the risk of blowing the engine.

Many times when an engine fails, the service contract administrator will not cover the repair until the dealership performs a thorough inspection, because it first wants to determine whether there was any misuse or abuse. A thorough inspection is often impossible without a *teardown* of the entire engine. And the administrator often requires the consumer to pay for this teardown in advance—an expense that many people cannot afford. But if they cannot pay for teardowns, then their claims are denied, and they do not receive the benefits they paid for when they bought their service contracts in the first place. This is hardly fair.

4. See chapter 11, 143, "Manufacturer Defenses."

Even where a complete teardown does occur, many times the inspection report will automatically blame the consumer for abuse, with little basis for that conclusion. After all, the defect is not covered, and it will save the service contract company thousands of dollars in repairs. If a consumer is not armed with an automotive expert to dispute this false finding, he or she will be at the mercy of unethical people.

Should I Buy a Service Contract?

The price of a service contract is typically based on several factors: the make and model of the vehicle; whether the vehicle is new or used; and the desired coverage and length of the service contract. The cost can range from several hundred dollars to over a thousand dollars or even more.

Some people will gladly pay for extra coverage for their vehicle, just for the comfort of knowing that defects will be taken care of no matter what happens. For people who keep a close eye on their budgets, service contracts make sense if they plan to put a lot of miles on their vehicles in a short period of time. In such cases, the original warranty will expire much sooner, so a service contract could be worth its weight in gold. Otherwise, the manufacturer's basic warranties are usually adequate.

Service Contract Questions and Answers

Does the service contract duplicate any warranty coverage?

Yes, but more often than not it provides less coverage than the manufacturer's warranty.

Who backs the service contract?

Find out who performs or pays for repairs under the terms of the service contract. It might be the manufacturer, the dealer, or an independent company.

How much does the service contract cost?

Usually, the price of the service contract is based on the car make and model, condition (new or used), coverage, and length of contract. The upfront cost can range from several hundred dollars to more than a thousand dollars.

What is covered and not covered?

Few auto service contracts cover all repairs. In fact, common repairs for parts like brakes and clutches generally are not included in service contracts. If a component is not listed in the contract, assume it is not covered.

How are claims handled?

When your car needs to be repaired or serviced, you may be able to choose among several service dealers or authorized repair centers. Or, you may be required to return the vehicle to the selling dealer for service.

What are your responsibilities?

Under the contract, you may have to follow all of the manufacturer's recommendations for routine maintenance, such as oil and spark plug changes. Failure to do so may void the contract. Keep detailed records, including receipts.

"As Is" Sale

Sometimes a motor vehicle, most commonly a used vehicle, is sold "as is" or "with all faults." Such vehicles usually do not come with any warranties at all, either express or implied.

Some state lemon laws—including California's—place limits on a dealer's right to sell a vehicle "as is." Ordinarily, however, the buyer is simply agreeing to take the vehicle in the condition it is in, regardless of what that condition may be. Consider carefully before buying a vehicle without the valuable protections that warranties can provide.

Be absolutely certain that you check the Buyer's Guide where the type of warranty for the car you want is shown. See figure 9.1 for a picture of a typical warranty page. Note the language at the very top of the form.

Figure 9.1. Buyer's Guide Warranty Page

BUYERS GUIDE

IMPORTANT: Spoken promises are difficult to enforce. Ask dealer to put all promises in writing. Keep this form.

_____ _____ _____ _____
VEHICLE MAKE   MODEL   YEAR   VIN

_____
DEALER STOCK NUMBER (optional)

WARRANTIES FOR THIS VEHICLE:

☐ **AS IS-NO WARRANTY**

YOU WILL PAY ALL COSTS FOR ANY REPAIRS. The dealer assumes no responsibility for any repairs regardless of any oral statements about this vehicle.

☐ **WARRANTY**

☐ **FULL** ☐ **LIMITED WARRANTY. The dealer will pay _____ % of the labor and _____% of the parts for the covered systems that fail during the warranty period. Ask the dealer for a copy of the warranty documents for a full explanation of warranty coverage, exclusions, and the dealer's repair obligations. Under state law, "implied warranties" may give you even more rights.**

SYSTEMS COVERED: **DURATION:**

_____   _____
_____   _____
_____   _____
_____   _____
_____   _____
_____   _____
_____   _____
_____   _____

☐ **SERVICE CONTRACT. A service contract is available at an extra charge on this vehicle. Ask for details as to coverage, deductible, price, and exclusions. If you buy a service contract within 90 days of the time of sale, state law "implied warranties" may give you additional rights.**

PRE PURCHASE INSPECTION: ASK THE DEALER IF YOU MAY HAVE THIS VEHICLE INSPECTED BY YOUR MECHANIC EITHER ON OR OFF THE LOT.

CHAPTER 10

Replacement or Refund: Choosing a Remedy

> *"Focus on remedies, not faults."*
> —Jack Nicklaus

Definition of Remedy

- Something that corrects an evil, fault, or error.

- A legal order that prevents or corrects a wrong or enforces a right.

We could not agree more with Jack Nicklaus. Don't sit in the misery of it all. Decide to seek help, and with experienced assistance you will have the remedy you deserve.

All the consumer ever wanted from day one was for the manufacturer and its dealers to correct the defect and let the consumer get on with his or her life.

For you, the consumer, remedies are those actions that manufacturers must take to correct the situation when they have sold you a lemon automobile.

Choosing a Remedy: Your Choice

You have several options:

- Return the vehicle for a refund

- Return the vehicle for a replacement

- Keep the vehicle and receive money

You are usually not limited to the remedy the dealer or manufacturer recommends. For example, if the manufacturer suggests that you must accept a replacement vehicle instead of a refund, in many states—including California—this is not true. You get to choose. I recommend that you consult a lemon law attorney to help you decide what is best for you.

Refund

If you elect to receive a refund, you are entitled to the full purchase price, which usually includes

- the down payment;

- all monthly payments made up to the present, including finance charges;

- the loan balance fully paid off—usually paid directly to your lender.

In many states, your refund may also include

- official fees and charges, such as sales tax and registration fees;

- other expenses reasonably incurred in connection with your defective vehicle, such as rental cars, towing, repairs, and storage.

Almost all states permit the manufacturer to deduct some allowance for your use of the vehicle. Some states allow a deduction only for miles driven up to the first repair attempt. This recognizes that the failure to repair the vehicle is the manufacturer's responsibility, and that being forced to continue using a lemon is not a valuable benefit. Other states permit a deduction for all miles driven. If the latter situation applies to you, you may wish to write your legislature and let them know how unfair this policy is.

Example of a Refund: California

A consumer has a three-year-old car.

- The vehicle had 112 miles at the time of purchase.

- The original selling price of the vehicle was $22,500.00. The consumer got a five-year loan.

- The taxes and license for the vehicle were $2,250.00, included in the amount financed.

- The consumer made a down payment of $5,000.00.

- The consumer made 36 payments at $340.00 each. There is a loan balance of $9,800.00.

- The consumer spent $650.00 on DMV registration, $320.00 on rental cars, and $150.00 on towing charges.

- The vehicle's total miles are 48,943. The consumer first returned the vehicle for repair at 5,765 miles.

In California, the manufacturer would refund

$5,000.00 + (36 X $340.00) = $17,240.00

to the consumer, plus $9,800.00 to the lender.

Note that the consumer does not get to add $2,250.00 for taxes and license, because that money was included in the amount financed.

California's lemon law calculates the offset for use by multiplying the purchase price of the vehicle by the mileage that the consumer put on the vehicle before first returning the vehicle for repair, divided by 120,000 miles. In this example, the manufacturer is entitled to an offset of

[(5,765 miles – 112 miles) / 120,000 miles] X $22,500.00 = $1,059.94.

Finally, the manufacturer will reimburse the consumer for registration, rental, and towing, for a total of $1,120.00.

The total amount the consumer will receive is $17,086.19, plus payoff of the loan. The manufacturer must also pay the consumer's attorney's fees.

Replacement

If you choose to receive a replacement vehicle, your new vehicle must be comparable to the vehicle being replaced. Ideally, it should be substantially identical in make, model, and options. The manufacturer must typically pay any sales tax and registration fees on your new vehicle.

If you have a loan, you can usually do what is called a *substitution of collateral*. You keep your existing loan, existing payments, and existing interest rate, with full credit for all payments you have made so far. You simply switch the vehicle to which the loan applies.

The manufacturer generally may not charge you an *upgrade charge* if your new vehicle is a more recent model. It is not your fault that the manufacturer delayed three years before replacing your vehicle, so you should not have to pay for the fact that the manufacturer no longer has another exactly identical vehicle from the same model year as your old vehicle.

The manufacturer may also have to reimburse you for incidental charges that you reasonably incurred in connection with your defective vehicle, such as rental cars, towing, repairs, and storage.

As with a refund, most states permit the manufacturer to deduct some allowance for your use of the vehicle.

Example of a Replacement

Using the same facts in the refund example, the consumer's three-year-old sedan has leather seats, a CD player, and a sunroof. The consumer would receive a brand-new current year sedan of the same make and model, with leather seats, a CD player, and a sunroof. The manufacturer would cover the sales tax and registration fees on the new vehicle.

The replacement vehicle would be substituted for the lemon vehicle on the loan. The consumer would continue monthly payments as normal.

The manufacturer would be entitled to $1,273.81 for the mileage offset. However, the manufacturer would also owe the consumer $1,120.00 for registration, towing, and rental cars. The consumer would have to pay only $153.81 for the replacement.

Rest assured that the manufacturer's representative will examine the vehicle carefully before returning you any of your money.

Return of Defective Vehicle

Whether you chose refund or replacement, you will generally be returning your lemon to the manufacturer. Most lemon laws expressly require the manufacturer to *accept return of the vehicle.* You must return it free from damage other than normal wear and tear.

> If your vehicle has any unusual damage, be sure to get it repaired before you try to return it. Otherwise, the manufacturer can charge you for the cost of repair, often at inflated dealer prices.

The Third Option

The consumer also has the right to choose neither refund nor replacement, and keep the vehicle even though it is defective. In such a case, the consumer would still be entitled to recover the difference between what the vehicle is worth with the defects and what it would have been worth without the defects.

> As a practical matter, buyers usually keep their vehicles only when the manufacturers mislead them into believing that they have no other choice.

Incidental and Consequential Damages

Incidental and consequential damages include any damages your state law allows you to recover that are not already part of the purchase price. These damages vary widely from state to state,[1] but may typically include

- sales tax

- license and registration fees

- interest and finance charges

- insurance premiums

- repair and maintenance costs

- rental car and travel expenses

- towing and storage charges

- loss of use

- personal injuries and property damage

- lost wages and profits contemplated at the time of sale.

---

1. See appendix A, Lemon Law Summary All Fifty States.

Incidental Damages

Incidental damages are expenses incident, or secondary, to the violation of warranty. These include items such as expenses reasonably incurred in connection with your continued possession of the defective vehicle.

Technically, it's the manufacturer's vehicle, and you are just stuck taking care of it for the manufacturer until the manufacturer finally takes it back. Thus, the manufacturer should have to pay you back for anything you spend taking care of its vehicle.

Typical incidental damages include taxes, registration fees, maintenance, storage, and repairs unrelated to any warranty defect.

Incidental: an award in a lawsuit for breach of contract in compensation for commercially reasonable expenses incurred as a result of the other party's breach, such as costs of inspecting and returning goods that do not conform to contract specifications.

Consequential Damages

Consequential damages are things that you have to pay for as a consequence, or result, of the defects. The manufacturer is responsible only for consequential damages that the seller knew or should have known would result from the defects.

Typical consequential damages include repair costs, towing, rental cars, loss of use, storage, and even business losses if the seller knew that you intended to use the goods for business. Because lemon law cases involve motor vehicles, other expenses are reasonably foreseeable, such as registration, insurance, accessories, and interest and finance charges on your car loan.

Consequential damages also include any injury to person, and any damage to property other than the vehicle itself. In these cases, it is not important whether anybody knew or should have known that the defects could cause the injury or damage. All that matters is that it resulted from the defects.

Note that some items, such as registration fees, may be both incidental damage and consequential damage.

Accessories

An accessory is anything that is not included on the vehicle when it leaves the factory. Sometimes the dealer may add accessories before selling the vehicle; sometimes the consumer may add accessories later. Common accessories include

- alarms

- stereos and CD players

- sunroofs

- trailer hitches

- special lights or lighting harnesses

- running boards

- navigation system

- hands-free telephone.

If you are going to return your vehicle to the manufacturer, the safest practice is to remove any accessories you can without damaging the vehicle. Manufacturers are rarely willing to reimburse you for accessories that they did not put on your vehicle.

On the other hand, if you cannot safely remove the accessories, a question arises: Why should the manufacturer get for free the accessories that you paid for with your money?

If the manufacturer were to repurchase a vehicle without paying for its accessories, the manufacturer would be getting more than it paid for, which would be unfair. In the law this is called *unjust enrichment*.

Here is another way to look at it. The consumer is returning the vehicle to the manufacturer only because of its defects. The seller should know, at the time of sale, that if you end up having to return the vehicle, you will also have to return any accessories that came with it. It follows that accessories that come with the vehicle are consequential damages.

The same reasoning should hold true even for accessories that the consumer adds after the sale. The consumer reasonably relies on the manufacturer's promise, in its warranty, that it will repair the vehicle and keep it free from defects. The consumer relies on that promise when buying accessories, not expecting that the vehicle will be a lemon. Thus, the loss of accessories is a consequence of the manufacturer's failure to keep its promise.

CHAPTER 11

Manufacturer Defenses

> *"It isn't making mistakes that's critical, it's correcting them and getting on with the principal task."*
> —Donald Rumsfeld

Introduction to Defenses

Lemon law statutes are now much stronger than they were even ten years ago. Still, not every consumer can successfully demand a refund under the lemon law, regardless of the nature of the defect.

The courts are well aware that some consumers are foolish enough to think they can blame their worn-out engine on a manufacturing defect or poor repairs at the dealership. Manufacturers have defenses against this sort of thing. Many of them are listed in your warranty.

He Said, She Said

Unfortunately, you will find that a manufacturer's first line of defense is often either denial or outright falsehood. The technicians who worked on your car—who have families to feed and therefore would like to keep their jobs—will develop sudden amnesia.

Service writers will claim you said things that you never said. Or they may claim you never said things that you know you did say. They will say they told you things that you know you never heard. How can a judge or jury know whom to believe?

The answer is the paper trail. Our world thrives on paper, on records, on documents. Whenever a dispute arises, the person who has the best paper trail stands the best chance of winning.

When your vehicle is repaired, never leave without your copy of the repair order. **Read it!** If there is something you do not understand, ask about it. If something is missing, point it out to the service writer. For example, if you went along on a test drive to demonstrate an abnormal front-end vibration, and the technician said, *"Yeah, I can feel that; that's not right,"* make sure the repair order reflects that the technician verified your complaint.

Most important of all, if anything in the repair order is even slightly inaccurate in any way, **do not sign it!** If you sign something without reading it, it will be presumed accurate, and you may lose the paper chase.

Don't forget, when you present your car for repair, it counts as a repair attempt regardless of whether the dealership actually tries to repair anything.[1] Make sure you get a repair order, even if nothing is done.

Driver Abuse

If a defect is the result of abuse, neglect, or unauthorized modifications or alterations, you will not be allowed to take advantage of the lemon law. The manufacturer generally bears the burden of proving abuse, neglect, or unauthorized modification or alteration.[2]

1. See chapter 8, 99, What Is a Lemon?
2. See chapter 8, 110, The Burden of Proof.

"No, Mr. Smith, I don't think this is what the manufacturer had in mind for this vehicle."

Vehicle Abuse

Suppose you have a Volkswagen Beetle. You decide to take a trip across country to visit friends. You need to take a few things with you, so you rent a two-ton trailer and hitch it to the back of the Beetle.

You arrive ten days later, engine overheating, brakes smoking, and rear shock absorbers shot. If you were to take the vehicle to the dealer and claim that it was a lemon because the engine, brakes, and shock absorbers failed, you wouldn't have a shock absorber to stand on.

Similarly, if the engine in your Honda Accord fails during an impromptu 120 mph drag race with a Ford station wagon, it would be considered vehicle abuse. If you were to go for a weekend of off-road fun in your Cadillac DeVille, this also wouldn't help you in a lemon law case.

Common sense is the rule. Vehicles are made for a purpose. Using them in a way that is inconsistent with this purpose may be considered abuse.

Keep in mind, however, that the alleged abuse must actually cause the defect in order to be a valid defense. For example, if the vehicle's seat belts won't stay latched, your off-road driving shouldn't matter.

Improper Maintenance

In not so many years, the backyard mechanic will be a relic. Modern vehicles are too complex and require tools the average owner cannot begin to afford.

You may consider yourself a good mechanic, and perhaps you are. However, if your dealer does not certify you, it is best that you do not perform maintenance on your vehicle while it is under warranty. If you decide to do oil changes and tune-ups on your own vehicle, you put yourself at risk if your vehicle turns out to be a lemon.

On the other hand, there is nothing that requires a consumer to have normal maintenance performed at the dealership. Be certain to keep complete records of all maintenance to show that proper care of the vehicle has been taken. This will help to eliminate any suggestion that defects are the result of improper maintenance.

The manufacturer will try to prove that whatever you did to the car is the real cause of any defect. Engine problem? It's because you didn't change the oil properly. The manufacturer bears the burden of proof—but why create an unnecessary issue?

Vehicle Neglect

Your owner's manual describes the kind of maintenance your vehicle needs, and how often it should be performed. Whether you agree with the service intervals or not, it is best to stick to the manufacturer's schedule as closely as possible. Otherwise, the manufacturer will try to blame your vehicle's defects on the lack of maintenance.

Modifications and Alterations

Americans love to add things to their cars. They love to modify them in ways that suit their individuality. There is risk in this. Adding a radical camshaft to the engine so that you can burn rubber for two hundred feet is an unauthorized modification. If something goes wrong with the vehicle, the manufacturer will certainly try to blame it on the modification.

Manufacturers can also raise this defense for seemingly harmless accessories. For example, if you add an upgraded CD player to your vehicle, and then start experiencing problems with the power door locks, dashboard indicators, and headlights, guess what the manufacturer is going to claim caused your electrical problems?

Voiding the Warranty

Take a close look at your warranty. It lists a number of things that can void the warranty, such as taking your vehicle to an unqualified repair shop. Know what these are. Don't give the manufacturer any excuse to void your warranty.

Statute of Limitations

A statute of limitations limits the time in which anyone can bring a lawsuit. People cannot bring lawsuits based on things that supposedly occurred decades ago. As time passes, memories fade, documents are discarded, and witnesses move away or even die. As a practical matter, some sensible limit must be placed on the right to take legal action.

The time limit for bringing a lemon lawsuit varies from state to state. Some states, including California, use the general four-year statute of limitations found in the Commercial Code. Other state lemon laws contain their own special statutes of limitations.[3]

The Discovery Rule

In some cases, the statute of limitations will say when it starts to run. For example, a state's lemon law might provide that the consumer must file a lemon lawsuit within three years from the date of purchase.

Other statutes of limitations do not define when they start to run. A lemon law may have a four-year statute of limitations, but not contain language specifying four years from what point. In these cases, the statute of limitations usually will not start to run until you *discover* the events that give you the right to file a lawsuit. This is called the *discovery rule*.

In a lemon law case, you do not have the right to file a lawsuit the day you buy your vehicle; nothing has gone wrong yet. When something does go wrong, you still have to give the manufacturer a reasonable number of attempts to fix the vehicle. Thus, in some states the statute of limitations is delayed until you *discover* that the manufacturer has had a reasonable number of repair attempts.

---

3. See appendix A, Lemon Law Summary All Fifty States.

In states that use the Commercial Code's statute of limitations, the discovery rule is reflected in the statute itself. The Commercial Code contains a four-year statute of limitations, which ordinarily runs from the time of sale. However, the rule is different if the action is based on a warranty that guarantees that the manufacturer will do something in the future.

Where a manufacturer promises to fix defects that appear after sale, that promise is not broken at the time of sale. It is not broken the first time a defect appears. It is broken when the manufacturer tries to fix the vehicle, but fails.

Thus, the four-year limit on filing a lawsuit does not begin to run until the consumer discovers the broken promise. That is, the statute of limitations does not begin to run until the consumer discovers—or reasonably should have discovered—that the manufacturer cannot or will not fulfill its obligations under warranty by successfully repairing the vehicle.

A Practical Example

Ms. Peter's story is a good illustration of how the discovery rule can work.[4] She purchased her used vehicle on April 20, 1999. She did not consult an attorney until May 15, 2003, more than four years later. Without the discovery rule, the four-year statute of limitations would have barred her lawsuit.

However, the dealer tried to repair her vehicle only once before October of 1999. The manufacturer was probably entitled to more than one attempt to fix the vehicle. The statute of limitations did not begin to run until after there had been a reasonable number of repair attempts.

The dealer kept trying to fix her vehicle through May of 2003. A lawsuit filed in, say, August of 2003 would be timely under the four-year statute of limitations, regardless of whether a jury ultimately decided that a reasonable number of repair attempts was two, six, or anything in between.

---

4. See chapter 3, 25, "A Used Car Lemon Story."

CHAPTER 12

Litigation

> *"Discourage litigation. Persuade your neighbors to compromise whenever you can. As a peacemaker the lawyer has superior opportunity of being a good man. There will still be business enough."*
> —Abraham Lincoln

Introduction to Litigation

Well, you made it this far. You gave the manufacturer a reasonable opportunity to repair. You survived the gauntlet. You learned about your rights and remedies under the lemon law. You are ready to proceed. What do you do next?

In some states you have no choice. You must submit your claim to an informal dispute resolution process. Even in states where arbitration is not mandatory, most manufacturers maintain some sort of informal dispute resolution process, and encourage you to use it before formal litigation.

To Arbitrate or Not to Arbitrate

There are basically three viewpoints from which to look at informal dispute resolution processes: the legal system, the manufacturer, and the consumer.

The Legislature and the Courts

It is an unfortunate fact that courts around the country are badly overloaded. The government, which has to fund the court system, loves the idea of arbitration, because it should save money and court time. This is the viewpoint that led Congress, when creating the Magnuson-Moss Act, to include a method for trying to resolve lemon law disputes informally, before litigation.[1]

Again, Congress did not deprive consumers of access to the courts. Under Magnuson-Moss, you do not have to accept the result of the informal dispute resolution process. You may take further legal action if you feel the result is inadequate or incorrect. Congress just wanted to encourage parties to try to resolve their disputes out of court.

Some state legislatures, including California's, have followed Congress's lead. These states encourage parties to try arbitration, without making it mandatory in every case. Other states have made it law that the consumer must use some *Dispute Resolution Settlement* process in a lemon law claim.[2] All of these state and federal efforts to provide alternatives to litigation have their roots in a desire to reduce the burden on our congested courts.

The Manufacturer and Arbitration

Manufacturers love any kind of arbitration. It is just another step in the gauntlet. Informal dispute resolution takes time. Any delay favors the manufacturer, who is not the one driving the defective vehicle. The manufacturer can also afford the expense, time, and travel necessary to attend the arbitration. The consumer may not be able to.

1. See chapter 4, 39, 1975: Federal Lemon Law.
2. See appendix A, Lemon Law Summary All Fifty States.

Consumers are frequently unfamiliar with the law, and with the arbitration process. This can lead to awards in favor of the manufacturer even where the facts are relatively clear. It probably does not help that the manufacturers themselves fund almost all of these so-called *independent* dispute resolution processes.

Far too often, manufacturers use the dispute resolution process or arbitration as just another step in the gauntlet.

The Consumer and Arbitration

Dispute resolution processes rarely benefit consumers. To begin with, the manufacturer's representatives will be well prepared. Consumers are severely hampered by their lack of familiarity with the law, and with the arbitration procedure. Even the arbitrators are not always as familiar with the lemon law as they should be—probably because they are not required to follow that law when issuing their decisions.

"Finally, Sandy, someone's going to listen."

"They listened all right, but not to me!"

Arbitrations waste time and money. Consumers cannot grasp the number of different ways arbitrations can go wrong. Even if they win, they rarely get the replacement or refund they deserve.[3]

If your state law does not require you to participate in an informal dispute resolution process, I recommend that you avoid it.

Before Litigation

Once you have decided to pursue your rights under the lemon law, it is important that you seek legal advice as soon as possible. You may think that I am saying this because I am an attorney myself. I am an attorney, but it does not change the fact that an attorney's assistance can be invaluable, even before filing a lawsuit.

Few people really know or understand their legal rights. Their knowledge of the law seldom extends beyond what they may have learned from watching television. They don't spend their valuable time and energy planning to do battle with giant corporations. They have better things to do.

We've said it many times and it bears repeating: do not give up and go away. The lemon law is for your protection. Make use of it.

Without an attorney, many consumers would give up and go away. This is just what manufacturers want. The people in the lemon stories chose to fight back. They sought legal representation to determine whether they had lemons. They hired attorneys so they could do something about it.

You might think of an attorney as an unrelenting aunt who accompanies a boy and girl on their first serious date. The boy pleads his case—or, these days, perhaps the girl does. Either way, the aunt reads the fine print and makes certain that everything is correct. Nothing occurs without her approval, and no one is going to do anything that he or she is not supposed to do. Inexperience is not going to get them into trouble.

3. See chapter 7, 95, Informal Dispute Resolution: Arbitration.

"Mr. and Mrs. Rodriguez, you have a strong case. Would you prefer a refund or a replacement vehicle?"

Selecting an Attorney

The practice of law, like medicine and science, is broad and specialized. You can find an experienced lawyer who specializes in the lemon law through the telephone directory or your local Bar Association.

If you have access to the Internet, there are several services that can help you locate an attorney for your specific needs in your area. These days, many attorneys have their own Web sites. If you do a search for *lemon law* or *lemon lawyers* on the Internet, you should find help.

Once you locate some lemon law attorneys, find out how long they have been doing this work. You are going to be working with them for some time, so you want to be comfortable with their skill and experience.

What Happens Before a Lawsuit Is Filed?

From my experience, most lemon law cases are settled without the need to take the manufacturer to court. Only 5–10 percent of lemon law cases go all the way to trial. The other 90–95 percent are settled either during litigation or before it.

> The first question of course is to determine if your vehicle is legally a lemon.

When you consult an attorney, the first thing to decide is whether your situation meets the standards of the applicable warranty laws. In other words, is your car legally a lemon?

Part of this determination may require you to retain an expert consultant to examine your vehicle and provide a professional opinion. Ask your attorney whether you need one.

The Paper Trail

Proper paperwork is vital to any lemon law claim.[4] At a minimum, you should have the following:

- Your purchase or lease contract

- All warranties, including any extended warranties or service contracts

- All other paperwork that you receive at the time of sale or lease

- All copies of all repair orders, even ones that may appear to be duplicates

- All service and maintenance records

- Any written communication between you and the manufacturer, or between you and any authorized dealer

- If you had to go through an informal dispute settlement process, all related documents

---

4. See chapter 11, 143, He Said, She Said.

The following documents may also be useful:

- Any photographs or videotapes you may have made of the problems with your vehicle

- Evidence of payments made, including statements from your lender and canceled checks

- DMV registration

- Receipts for towing, rental cars, storage, and other incidental expenses

The old adage of a picture being worth a thousand words is really true.

Notifying the Manufacturer

Once your attorney determines that your vehicle is a lemon, the next step is to give notice to the manufacturer. Many states require a particular form of written notice before you can pursue all of your rights under the lemon law.

In some states, the manufacturer must respond in a certain way to a proper written notice. In others, however, the manufacturer may treat your written notice as an invitation to start the gauntlet all over again.

Manufacturer's Responses

Here are a few of the devices the manufacturer may use to draw out the process:

> The written notice will be ignored.

The manufacturer would like you to think that it is not bothering to respond because you clearly have no case. If your attorney sends a written notice, it is because the attorney knows you have a case.

> The manufacturer may tell you that you do not qualify.

This is particularly common if you send a notice without an attorney. The manufacturer may think it can get away with this because of your inexperience. Don't listen!

> You will get the *glad hand*, followed by no real action.[5] Or you may be offered another repair.

Some states require you to allow the manufacturer one more repair attempt after you have given written notice. Other states, like California, do not.

> You may be offered a certificate toward the purchase of another of the manufacturer's products.

Why would you want another vehicle from the company that just took you through the gauntlet?

> You may be offered two or three months of car payments, in exchange for a signed release of all claims against the manufacturer.

Never sign this! If you sign, you will never be able to sue the manufacturer, regardless of whether you have a case.[6]

> The manufacturer will attempt to refer you to a dispute settlement process.

The manufacturer isn't interested in justice through the dispute settlement process. It knows that arbitration will simply consume time and money, and that you almost certainly will not get what you deserve.[7]

> The manufacturer will offer you something, but less than the law allows.

---

5. See chapter 7, 91, The *Glad Hand*.
6. See chapter 7, 93, Just Sign This Release, Mr. and Mrs. Jones.
7. See chapter 7, 95, Informal Dispute Resolution: Arbitration.

Beware of *good deals*. The manufacturer knows what you are entitled to under the lemon law, but it is still watching the bottom line. Every dollar it doesn't pay you is a dollar saved.

> The manufacturer may make you a verbal offer that sounds just like what you want to hear.

Never accept any deal that is not in writing. Otherwise, when it comes time for the actual settlement, the manufacturer may claim that it never promised what you say it promised. The manufacturer is lying, but it is very difficult to prove when you don't have anything in writing. If, at the time of the verbal offer, you ask for it in writing and the manufacturer refuses, it was never a serious offer.

> The manufacturer may actually agree to replace or repurchase your vehicle.

Instead of the manufacturer doing the right thing,
it can seem more like a hostage exchange.

> The manufacturer may reject the demand.

Attorneys' Fees: Can I Afford to Sue?

Whenever legal issues arise, ordinary people generally have the idea that attorneys' fees are unaffordable. Once, only wealthy people and corporations could afford to pay the hourly rates of attorneys. Under the lemon laws in many states, this is no longer true.

There is nothing more powerful than a person who knows he is right, and who will not back off from that position.

Many lemon laws make it easier for purchasers to sue corporations by allowing them to recover court costs and reasonable attorneys' fees. This means that if the manufacturer loses a lemon lawsuit, it may have to pay the consumer's costs of bringing suit, including lawyers' fees.

Why Consumers Can Recover Attorneys' Fees

Lemon laws allow the consumer to receive either a refund for the value of the vehicle, or replacement with a comparable vehicle. However, a trial can easily cost $15,000 to $75,000, or even more. Most consumers cannot afford to pay that kind of money.

One way that consumers can avoid having to pay their attorneys up front is by using what is called a contingency fee agreement. Traditionally, this means that the attorney is not paid by the hour, but instead agrees to take a portion of the client's ultimate recovery—if the client wins. A typical percentage might be one-third of the total recovery. If the client loses, neither the client nor the attorney receives anything. Both the risk and the reward are shared.

Contingency: a fee for an attorney's services that is payable only in the event of a successful or satisfactory outcome.

Contingency arrangements work as long as attorneys are able to balance their potential recovery against the time they must put in on the case. If the client's damages are potentially large, the attorney's time and effort may be well rewarded if the client prevails. On the other hand, if a case appears to be very time consuming for a comparatively small return, few if any lawyers will offer their services on contingency, even for a valid case.

The traditional contingency agreement does not work well in a lemon law case. The consumers have to give up a portion of their recovery, which is hardly fair. And, because nowadays an average vehicle costs only about $25,000 to $30,000, the lawyers get a fraction of the work they actually invest in the case.

It is hardly fair for consumers to end up with less than they paid for their vehicles.

For example, if the agreement were for one-third of the consumer's recovery, and the value of the defective vehicle were $27,000, then the consumer would receive $18,000, and the attorney would be paid only $9,000. Under a contingency agreement, neither consumers nor lawyers get what they deserve.

If the law provided no alternative to this situation, there would be no incentive for attorneys to handle lemon law cases at all. Even the strongest lemon laws are useless without tough, determined attorneys prepared to do battle with auto manufacturers on behalf of consumers. Very few consumers are willing to take the risk, or able to pay an attorney by the hour, when such potentially high costs are at stake. And even fewer attorneys can afford to spend $75,000 on a case and collect $9,000 in fees.

Many state and federal lawmakers recognized this problem. As a result, many lemon laws, including California's, permit the consumer to recover attorney fees in addition to a replacement or refund. Once you prevail—whether by settlement or by winning the lawsuit at trial—the manufacturer, and not you, can be required to pay your attorney's fees.

Not all state lemon laws include a provision for attorneys' fees. However, even in those states, you can still recover your fees by bringing a lawsuit under the federal Magnuson-Moss Act—which does have such a provision—instead of under your local lemon law. Again, consult with your attorney if you have any concerns.

Shifting the Burden of Attorneys' Fees

Some lemon laws, including California's, award attorney fees to a consumer who wins a case, but not to a manufacturer even if it successfully defends itself. This is called a fee-shifting provision, because it shifts the burden of attorney fees to one party only.

Fee-shifting provisions put consumers on an equal footing with manufacturers. They create an incentive for attorneys to represent consumers, knowing that if they prevail they will be paid for their efforts.

The law must serve all the people, rich and poor alike, and not just massive corporations that can afford to keep attorneys on retainer year in and year out. An award of attorneys' fees in such cases is the great equalizer in the lemon law.

If Mr. Jones owns an inexpensive vehicle that cost him only $15,000, he can still afford to retain the services of an attorney who practices lemon law. He will not have to pay vast sums of money to keep his case going against a manufacturer with seemingly endless resources, both in lawyers and in funds.

If a manufacturer is foolish enough to force a consumer who has a genuine lemon to take a case all the way to trial, it will drive up the fees of the consumer's attorney. In addition to ultimately giving the consumer a refund, the manufacturer will have to pay that attorney's fees.

Litigation

When you arrive at this point in a lemon law case, it should be because you have tried every other avenue. It will also be because you have not given in and gone away, as the manufacturers tried so hard to make you do.

How Long Will It Take?

It is very difficult to say how long a particular lemon law case will take, as each case is different due to the manufacturer, the age of the vehicle, its mileage, the nature of defects, and the number of repairs. While some cases settle in prelitigation in as little as thirty days or less, cases that go to trial can last up to two years or more. On average, most cases that go to litigation probably last at least a year.

What Do I Have to Show in Court?

In a lemon law case, a consumer must usually present evidence of the following things to the court:

- A sales contract or lease

- A written warranty

- One or more defects

- Substantial impairment in use, value, or safety

- The manufacturer's reasonable number of attempts to repair the vehicle[8]

Jury instructions will set forth all of the elements that you must prove in order to win. Your attorney will discuss each of these elements with you, long before you get to trial.

The typical juror knows as little about cars as you do. Thus, the testimony of an experienced automotive expert is usually invaluable in helping you prove your case. The manufacturer will certainly offer expert testimony from at least one of its own technical people. Your attorney may be able to recommend an expert for you to hire.

---

8. See chapter 8, 99, "How Can I Tell If My Vehicle Is a Lemon?"

Discovery

In the course of your lawsuit, you will probably have to participate in some form of discovery. *Discovery* is the legal term for each party's right to learn things from the other side. This includes the right to ask questions, request documents, or inspect property.

In a typical lemon law case, the manufacturer will want to take your deposition. In a deposition, the manufacturer's attorney asks you questions, which you must answer under oath. Your attorney will be present to protect you against improper questioning.

The manufacturer will probably also demand an inspection of your vehicle. Your expert should attend any defense inspection, to protect your interests. Manufacturers may also send written discovery to you, demanding that you answer written questions, produce documents, and things like that. Your attorney will help you respond to these demands.

Your attorney may also take depositions, demand documents, and send written questions to the manufacturer. Both sides have the same right to conduct discovery in any lawsuit.

What Is a Settlement Conference?

Just because you have had to file a lawsuit does not mean you will definitely go all the way to trial. As mentioned earlier, the vast majority of lemon law cases settle before trial. Your attorney will continue to try to resolve your lawsuit throughout the entire litigation process.

One way that courts encourage parties to try to settle their disputes, even after filing a lawsuit, is to have them participate in a settlement conference or mediation. In a settlement conference, an experienced legal professional— usually a judge, retired judge, or attorney—listens to both sides of a dispute, then tries to get the parties to agree on a resolution.

A settlement conference is not arbitration. It is not binding on either side. A mediator cannot force the manufacturer to repurchase your car, but a mediator also cannot force you to take less than you deserve. Mediation can resolve a case only if everyone agrees.

Civil Penalty

California's lemon law has a special provision for something called a *civil penalty*. The lemon laws of a few other states have similar provisions. The civil penalty is an additional penalty, beyond actual damages, that can be imposed on manufacturers for failure to comply with the lemon law. In California, it can be up to two times the consumer's actual damages.

Surprisingly, the primary purpose of the civil penalty is not to punish the manufacturer. Its purpose is to encourage manufacturers to comply with the lemon law voluntarily, rather than forcing consumers to file lawsuits.

With no possibility of a civil penalty, a manufacturer might be tempted to deny relief and make the consumer file a lawsuit, even where the vehicle is clearly a lemon. After all, what has the manufacturer got to lose? The consumer might give up and go away. He or she might be willing to accept less, to avoid the hassle of litigation. The jury might even decide in the manufacturer's favor for some reason.

The civil penalty puts sharp teeth in California's lemon law. It is a sad commentary on corporate ethics that such damages are necessary to hold manufacturers to a decent standard of behavior.

Even if the worst happened, and the manufacturer lost at trial, the manufacturer would pay only the same refund it should have paid all along. The manufacturer has no real incentive not to force the consumer to go through the litigation. It's just more of the gauntlet.

In states with civil penalties, the manufacturer faces a much more unpleasant prospect if it loses at trial. The threat of having to pay two or three times as much is a strong incentive for manufacturers to settle lemon law claims voluntarily. The consumers get what they deserve, no less, and the manufacturers pay what they owe, no more. Everybody wins.

If more lemon laws included civil penalty provisions, manufacturers might hesitate a little more before putting consumers through the full gauntlet. The only other thing that can negate the gauntlet is an informed public. I hope this book has that effect.

CHAPTER 13

Lemon Laundering

> *"Every crime depends on somebody not waking up too soon."*
> —G. K. Chesterton

What Is Laundering?

Laundering is the act of taking something dirty and making it clean. Money received from the sale of illicit drugs is frequently laundered to make it appear as though it were legitimately earned. It is an illegal activity and carries heavy penalties.

Lemon Vehicle Laundering

By now you know what a lemon is. You may even be driving one. In chapter 10, you learned that a manufacturer must either repurchase your lemon or replace it with a comparable vehicle. Either way, the manufacturer is stuck with a car that has been through numerous failed repair attempts. The vehicle may be entirely unsafe to drive.

Once you get rid of your lemon, the last thing you want is for someone else to be stuck with it, having no idea that it is a lemon.

Many states require the manufacturer to *brand* the title of the vehicle, permanently, with a notation such as *lemon law buyback*, so that subsequent purchasers will know about the vehicle's history. The vehicle is now just an expensive piece of junk, a loss. The manufacturer's only legitimate options are to try to repair the car again, or to destroy it. Unfortunately this is where criminal enterprise sometimes enters the picture.

Many times, the manufacturer or dealer simply sells lemon vehicles at auction, "as is." The auction company is usually located in another state, where the lemon law is different. Ideally—for the manufacturer—it will be in a state that does not require any sort of branding, and offers no protection to future purchasers. These states usually do not recognize title notations from other states.

It can hurt them, perhaps permanently.

The vehicle is retitled in the name of the auction company, and then retitled again in the name of the dealership—often from yet another state—that purchases it at auction. In the process, any notation that was once on the title disappears. The title to the car has been *washed* or *laundered*. The dealership at the end of the chain then sells the lemon as an ordinary used vehicle to some unsuspecting buyer.

Just as laundered money appears to be untainted, so does the laundered lemon vehicle. The new owner—who thinks he or she is getting a low mileage, relatively new car for an excellent price—may in fact be signing a death warrant. At the very least, some unsuspecting purchaser is about to enter the gauntlet again.

Isolated Cases or Big Business?

The number of damaged cars being resold is staggering. According to the National Association of Independent Insurers, approximately two and a half million vehicles in any given year are so badly damaged in accidents that they are declared total losses. Nevertheless, roughly 40 percent are rebuilt and put back on the road. Of this number, as many as one hundred thousand may be repurchased lemons, according to Consumers for Auto Reliability and Safety (CARS), a consumer watchdog group in California.[1]

To combat the problem of lemon laundering, many states—including California—have enacted statutes that require certain disclosures to subsequent buyers of lemon vehicles.

Buybacks Are Different

State laws classify a few types of used vehicles as worthy of special notice: salvage vehicles that are rebuilt from wrecks, flood-damaged cars, and lemon law buybacks. These vehicles have traits that separate them from ordinary used vehicles. In particular, they are more likely to have latent defects.

---

1. Refer to Web site Consumers for Auto Reliability and Safety at http://www.carconsumers.com.

> Latent defects are defects that are not apparent when the car is first purchased but appear some time later.

Under many state laws, a consumer buying a used lemon law buyback is entitled to notice of the history of problems that the first buyer experienced. These disclosures usually do not advise them of any existing defects, but only of the vehicle's history of problems. The disclosure provisions are designed to alert prospective purchasers that the first owner experienced serious problems with the vehicle.

A vehicle's history as a lemon law buyback is significant for several reasons. Cars with repeated problems, or that are out of service for extended periods, may have underlying structural or design flaws. They may be repaired with parts or components that have the same design flaws that caused the original problems. And they usually have a much lower resale value.

Consumers need to know when a vehicle has a history of defects and may be unsafe, unreliable, or very costly to operate and repair. Lemon law disclosures advise consumers of possible latent defects in the used vehicles they are thinking of buying. This information helps consumers make informed decisions, and also prevents fraud.

A Lemon Is a Lemon Is a Lemon

The lemon laundering problem is not limited to just those vehicles that are formally determined to be lemons in a lawsuit. It includes all vehicles with a history of defects, or known to the manufacturer to be substantially defective. It includes so-called goodwill buybacks and *trade assists* completed with financial assistance from the manufacturer or its financial arm (such as GMAC, which is affiliated with GM).

It doesn't matter whether the manufacturer bought back the vehicle due to an arbitration award, a court order, or so-called customer satisfaction. It doesn't matter what the manufacturer calls it. If it's a lemon, any potential secondary owner who might end up with the vehicle should be warned. Lives may well hang in the balance.

Some states, including California, already require title branding and resale disclosure even for goodwill buybacks, in which the manufacturer has never formally acknowledged an obligation to take back the vehicle.

Trade Assists

A *trade assist* means that the owner trades in a defective vehicle to the selling dealer for a new vehicle. Lemon owners may be desperate to get rid of their vehicles. As a result, they are sometimes induced to pay for a more expensive model, instead of choosing a replacement or refund as the lemon laws provide.[2]

At the very least, these trades should be made on terms more favorable to the consumer than a typical early trade-in, which can involve considerable depreciation. However, that is generally not the case. If anything, consumers can end up owing more after a trade assist than they owed on their original defective vehicle.

Manufacturers claim that trade assists simply promote *customer satisfaction*. They are not repurchases under a lemon law, or for some acknowledged defect. Manufacturers argue that, like goodwill buybacks, trade assists should not count as lemon law buybacks.

2. See chapter 7, 90, Dealer Offers to Sell You a New Car.

CA vs. Chrysler and Manufacturer Buybacks

As an excellent example of a manufacturer's misuse of the terms *goodwill* and *customer satisfaction,* consider the 1996 administrative action in California against Chrysler Corporation regarding the disposition of 119 repurchased vehicles. Chrysler contended that all 119 vehicles had been *customer satisfaction* buybacks, and thus not subject to the title branding, disclosure, and warranty requirements of California's lemon law.

But Chrysler's own statements and records acknowledged that the vehicles were actually lemon law buybacks. To begin with, Chrysler had repurchased 48 of the 119 vehicles following decisions in favor of the consumers in Chrysler's own dispute resolution process.

In addition, Chrysler had applied to the state for a sales tax refund under the lemon law for 115 of the 119. One sales tax refund request stated that the vehicle in question was a "State Lemon Law Buyback . . . Vehicle in four times for four attempts and thirty-two days down for repairs to transmission and brakes."

Of these 119 vehicles, 96 percent had safety defects. Their problems included faulty brakes that repeatedly caused harrowing incidents, transmissions that intermittently failed to shift above low gear in freeway traffic, and vehicles that unpredictably stalled on the freeway. Chrysler disclosed none of these serious safety hazards to the subsequent buyers.

The California DMV ultimately rejected Chrysler's excuses, and decided to bar Chrysler from delivering cars and trucks to the state for sixty days. The decision never went into effect, because Chrysler's dealers pointed out that it would penalize them for something that they didn't do. Even so, the dispute called attention to the widespread problem of lemon laundering.

Permanent Labeling

California was the first state to require a permanently affixed label on the driver's doorframe. A permanent decal identifies a lemon law buyback to prospective purchasers throughout the entire chain of ownership. If nothing else, this ensures that California consumers know when they are purchasing such a vehicle, even if the title has been washed in another state.

While some other states require window stickers that are more conspicuous, the lemon label that California requires is intended to be permanent. The law prohibits its removal. The costs are minimal, and are one-time only.

A permanent label also serves a useful purpose for auction companies and dealers. Vehicles are naturally transportable, and lemon vehicles may undergo several wholesale transactions before being resold to a retail consumer. A permanent decal indicates that additional paperwork and disclosures are required in connection with that vehicle, making it easier to comply with state lemon disclosure laws.

What Can You Do About It?

Before purchasing a used car, investigate. Find the Vehicle Identification Number (VIN), which should be on the window sticker. You can also find it on the top of the dashboard at the base of the windshield, on the driver's side. It is a string of seventeen letters and numbers.

Once you have the VIN, there are a number of ways to research the vehicle's title history. For example, for a small fee you can get a title history of the vehicle you want to purchase from CARFAX Vehicle History Reports, AutoCheck, Consumer Guide, and others.

And don't forget to check the left front doorframe for the *lemon law buyback decal.*

APPENDIX A

Lemon Law Summary
All Fifty States

Alabama—Ala. Code § 8-20A-1 et seq.	
Vehicles Covered:	New, self-propelled vehicles under 10,000 pounds, intended primarily for operation on public highways. Excludes motor homes.
Persons Covered:	Purchaser, any person entitled to enforce warranty.
Use Covered:	Vehicle used in substantial part for personal, family, or household purposes.
Defects Covered:	Defect significantly impairs use, value, or safety of vehicle, and arises solely during ordinary use of vehicle.
Period Covered:	Defect must first occur, and consumer must give notice of defect, within one year or 12,000 miles, whichever is first. Manufacturer must repair within two years or 24,000 miles, whichever is first.
Notice Requirement:	Written notice, by certified mail, describing vehicle, defects, and all attempts to correct defects, and demanding repair. Manufacturer entitled to final repair attempt after notice.
"Reasonable" Repair Guidelines:	Within two years or 24,000 miles, whichever is first, either at least three repairs to same defect, plus one final attempt by manufacturer, or at least 30 calendar days out of service for repairs. Creates presumption.
Affirmative Defenses:	Defect does not significantly impair use, market value, or safety of vehicle, or results from abuse, neglect, or unauthorized modification or alteration by consumer. Statute of limitations: three years from delivery.
Available Remedy:	Replacement or refund, at consumer's option.
Refund Details:	Full contract price; non-refundable portion of service contract; sales tax, license and registration fees, and similar charges; finance charges incurred after defect first reported; reasonable cost of alternative transportation and other incidental damages. Deduction for consumer's use before defect first reported.
Other Remedies:	Mandatory reasonable attorneys' fees to consumer. No limit on other consumer remedies.
Arbitration:	If manufacturer maintains informal settlement procedure, consumer must use before filing suit.
Resale of Lemon:	Disclosure required; title branded.

Alaska—Alaska Stat. § 45.45.300 et seq.

Vehicles Covered:	Self-propelled motorized land vehicles. Excludes tractors, farm vehicles, and off-road vehicles.
Persons Covered:	Original purchaser of new vehicle, or subsequent transferee.
Use Covered:	Vehicle normally used for personal, family, or household purposes.
Defects Covered:	Defect caused by manufacturer or its agents that prevents vehicle from being operated, makes vehicle unsafe to operate, or substantially decreases dollar value of vehicle.
Period Covered:	Warranty term or one year, whichever is first.
Notice Requirement:	Written notice by certified mail, no later than 60 days after period covered, describing defect, stating that a reasonable number of repair attempts have been made, and demanding refund or replacement. Manufacturer entitled to final repair attempt after notice.
"Reasonable" Repair Guidelines:	Within period covered, either at least three repairs to same defect or at least 30 business days out of service for repairs. Creates presumption.
Affirmative Defenses:	Defect does not substantially impair use or market value of vehicle, or results from unauthorized alteration, abuse, or neglect.
Available Remedy:	Replacement or refund, at consumer's option.
Refund Details:	Full purchase price, including registration fees and other costs added to price; reimbursement for cost of shipping vehicle to and from repair facility. Deduction for use of vehicle from date of delivery to original owner, not to exceed depreciation in value.
Other Remedies:	No limit on other consumer remedies. Failure to refund or replace is unfair trade practice.
Arbitration:	If manufacturer maintains informal settlement procedure, or offers in writing, after receipt of consumer's notice, to participate in qualified arbitration or mediation process, consumer must participate before entitled to replacement or refund.
Resale of Lemon:	Disclosure required.

American Samoa—Am. Samoa Code § 27.0701 et seq.

Vehicles Covered:	All automobiles and major appliances worth over $150.
Persons Covered:	Any consumer purchaser.
Use Covered:	Goods purchased primarily for personal, family, or household purposes and not for commercial or business use.
Defects Covered:	Any defect.
Period Covered:	Warranty term.
Notice Requirement:	None required.
"Reasonable" Repair Guidelines:	None; repairs must be achieved in reasonably short period of time.
Affirmative Defenses:	None specified.
Available Remedy:	Replacement or refund, at seller's option. If replacement, must be achieved in reasonably short period of time.
Refund Details:	Cash refund of value goods would have had at time of return if not defective.
Other Remedies:	None specified.
Arbitration:	None.
Resale of Lemon:	No disclosure required.

Arizona—Ariz. Rev. Stat. § 44-1261 et seq.	
Vehicles Covered:	New, self-propelled vehicles not over 10,000 pounds. Excludes living portions of motor homes.
Persons Covered:	Purchaser, transferee during express warranty term, or any person entitled to enforce warranty.
Use Covered:	Vehicle primarily designated for transportation of persons or property over public highways.
Defects Covered:	Defect that substantially impairs use and value of vehicle to consumer.
Period Covered:	Defect must first occur, and consumer must give notice of defect, within warranty term, two years, or 24,000 miles, whichever is first.
Notice Requirement:	Written notice of alleged defect, directly to manufacturer. Manufacturer entitled to final repair attempt after notice. If no notice, no presumption of reasonable number of repair attempts.
"Reasonable" Repair Guidelines:	Within period covered, either same defect repaired at least four times or at least 30 calendar days out of service for repairs. Creates presumption if above notice given.
Affirmative Defenses:	Defect does not substantially impair use and market value of vehicle, or is result of abuse, neglect, or unauthorized modification or alteration. Statute of limitations: six months from end of period covered.
Available Remedy:	Replacement or refund.
Refund Details:	Full purchase price, including all collateral charges. Deduction for use before first written notice of defect, and for all subsequent time when vehicle is not being repaired.
Other Remedies:	Mandatory reasonable costs and attorney's fees to consumer. No limit on other consumer remedies.
Arbitration:	If manufacturer maintains informal settlement procedure, consumer must use before entitled to refund or replacement.
Resale of Lemon:	Disclosure required.

Arkansas—Ark. Code § 4-90-401 et seq.	
Vehicles Covered:	Self-propelled vehicles not over 10,000 pounds. Excludes motorcycles, mopeds, and living portions of motor homes. Includes rest of motor home regardless of weight.
Persons Covered:	Original purchaser or lessee, or any person entitled to enforce warranty.
Use Covered:	Vehicle primarily designed for transportation of persons or property over public streets and highways.
Defects Covered:	Defect that substantially impairs use, market value, or safety, or does not conform to express warranty or implied warranty of merchantability.
Period Covered:	Two years or 24,000 miles.
Notice Requirement:	After three repairs for same defect, or one repair for serious safety defect, written notice to manufacturer, by certified mail, of need to repair defect. Manufacturer entitled to final repair attempt after notice.
"Reasonable" Repair Guidelines:	Three repairs for same defect—or one attempt to repair serious safety defect—plus one final opportunity for manufacturer to repair after notice; or at least 30 calendar days out of service for repairs; or at least five repairs for defects that together substantially impair vehicle. Creates presumption, but if manufacturer does not make final repair attempt after notice, conclusively establishes reasonable number of repair attempts.
Affirmative Defenses:	Defect does not impair use, value, or safety of vehicle, or is result of accident, abuse, neglect, or unauthorized modification or alteration; or consumer's claim not filed in good faith. Statute of limitations: two years from first report of defect, or from start of settlement procedure if used.
Available Remedy:	Replacement or refund. Consumer has right to choose refund.
Refund Details:	Full purchase or lease price; collateral charges, such as sales tax, finance charges, and charges for extended warranty; incidental charges, such as towing charges, rental costs, cost of alternative transportation. Deduction for use before first repair attempt.
Other Remedies:	Mandatory costs, expenses, and attorney's fees to consumer. No limit on other consumer remedies. Violation is deceptive trade practice.
Arbitration:	Manufacturer must maintain informal settlement proceeding, and must give consumer written notice, at time of purchase or lease, explaining consumer's rights and obligations under lemon law, including requirement that consumer give written notice of defect. If manufacturer does, consumer must use proceeding before bringing legal action.
Resale of Lemon:	Disclosure required; one-year/12,000-mile warranty.

California—Cal. Civ. Code § 1790 et seq.

Vehicles Covered:	All goods sold with warranties. Some provisions apply only to "new motor vehicles," which includes dealer-owned vehicles, demonstrators, and any other vehicle sold with original "new car" warranty, and excludes motorcycles, living portion of motor homes, and off-road vehicles.
Persons Covered:	Individual buyer or lessee, and any entity to which not more than five vehicles are registered in state.
Use Covered:	Vehicles used, bought, or leased for use primarily for personal, family, or household purposes, or primarily for business purposes if by an entity to which not more than five vehicles are registered in state.
Defects Covered:	Defect that substantially impairs use, value, or safety of vehicle to buyer or lessee.
Period Covered:	18 months or 18,000 miles, whichever is first.
Notice Requirement:	Direct notice to manufacturer of need for repair, but only if manufacturer clearly and conspicuously disclosed provisions of lemon law, including requirement of notice. If no notice, no presumption of reasonable number of repair attempts.
"Reasonable" Repair Guidelines:	Within period covered, at least four repairs to same defect, or at least two repairs to same serious safety defect, or more than 30 calendar days out of service for repairs. Creates presumption if above notice given (or not required).
Affirmative Defenses:	Defect caused by unauthorized or unreasonable use of vehicle following sale or lease. Statute of limitations: four years from discovery that manufacturer cannot or will not repair vehicle, extended while using third-party dispute resolution process.
Available Remedy:	Replacement or restitution. Consumer may choose restitution.
Refund Details:	Full purchase price, including sales tax, license and registration fees; other incidental damages, including reasonable repair, towing, and rental car costs actually incurred. Deduction for use before first repair attempt.
Other Remedies:	Possible civil penalty up to twice actual damages for certain violations. Mandatory costs, expenses, and attorney's fees to consumer. No limit on other consumer remedies.
Arbitration:	If manufacturer maintains qualified third-party dispute resolution process and timely notifies consumer in writing of its operation and effect, consumer must use process before invoking presumption.
Resale of Lemon:	Disclosure required; title branded; one-year warranty.

Colorado—Colo. Rev. Stat. § 42-10-101 et seq.	
Vehicles Covered:	Passenger vehicles sold in state, including pickup trucks and vans. Excludes vehicles that carry more than ten persons, motor homes, and vehicles with three or fewer wheels.
Use Covered:	Vehicle normally used for personal, family, or household purposes.
Defects Covered:	Defect that substantially impairs use and market value of vehicle.
Persons Covered:	Purchaser, transferee during express warranty term, and any person entitled to enforce warranty.
Period Covered:	Warranty term or one year, whichever is first.
Notice Requirement:	Written notice by certified mail, on form that manufacturer must provide in owner's manual. Manufacturer entitled to final repair attempt after notice. If no notice, no presumption of reasonable number of repair attempts.
"Reasonable" Repair Guidelines:	Within period covered, either at least four repairs to same defect or at least 30 business days out of service for repairs. Creates presumption if above notice given.
Affirmative Defenses:	Defect does not substantially impair use and market value of vehicle, or results from consumer's abuse, neglect, or unauthorized modifications or alterations. Statute of limitations: one year from delivery or six months from end of warranty, whichever is first, extended if informal settlement procedure used.
Available Remedy:	Replacement or refund, at manufacturer's option.
Refund Details:	Full purchase price, including sales tax, license and registration fees, and similar government charges. Deduction for use before first written notice of defect—including any use by prior owner—and for all subsequent time when vehicle is not being repaired.
Other Remedies:	Mandatory reasonable attorney's fees to prevailing party, whether consumer or manufacturer. No limit on other consumer remedies.
Arbitration:	If manufacturer maintains informal settlement procedure, consumer must use before entitled to refund or replacement.
Resale of Lemon:	No disclosure required.

Connecticut—Conn. Gen. Stat. § 42-179 et seq.	
Vehicles Covered:	New vehicles and motorcycles sold or leased in state.
Persons Covered:	Purchaser, lessee, transferee during express warranty term, or any person entitled to enforce warranty.
Use Covered:	Passenger motor vehicle, or passenger and commercial motor vehicle.
Defects Covered:	Defect that substantially impairs use, safety, or value of vehicle to consumer.
Period Covered:	Two years or 24,000 miles, whichever is first.
Notice Requirement:	Written notice of defect, if manufacturer clearly and conspicuously discloses notice requirement.
"Reasonable" Repair Guidelines:	Within period covered, either at least four repairs to same defect or at least 30 calendar days out of service for repairs. Alternately, within warranty term or one year, whichever is first, at least two repairs to same serious safety defect. Creates presumption.
Affirmative Defenses:	Defect does not substantially impair use, safety, or value of vehicle to consumer, or results from abuse, neglect, or unauthorized modifications or alterations by consumer.
Available Remedy:	Replacement if consumer accepts, or refund.
Refund Details:	Full purchase price, including transportation, preparation, and options; collateral charges, including sales tax, license and registration fees, and other government charges; finance charges after first report of defect; and incidental damages. Deduction for use before manufacturer's acceptance of vehicle's return.
Other Remedies:	Court may award costs and reasonable attorney's fees to consumer. Reasonable attorney's fees to manufacturer if action frivolous or in bad faith. No limit on other consumer remedies. Violation is unfair trade practice.
Arbitration:	If manufacturer maintains informal settlement procedure, consumer must use before entitled to refund or replacement. Even if not, consumer may still elect to submit dispute to binding arbitration.
Resale of Lemon:	Disclosure required; title branded.

Delaware—6 Del. Code § 5001 et seq.	
Vehicles Covered:	New vehicles sold, leased, or registered in state. Excludes motorcycles and living facilities of motor homes.
Persons Covered:	Purchaser, transferee during express warranty term, and any person entitled to enforce warranty.
Use Covered:	Passenger vehicle.
Defects Covered:	Defect that substantially impairs use, value, or safety of vehicle.
Period Covered:	One year or warranty term, whichever is first.
Notice Requirement:	Direct written notice to manufacturer. Manufacturer entitled to final repair attempt after notice.
"Reasonable" Repair Guidelines:	Within period covered, either at least four repairs to same defect or more than 30 calendar days out of service for repairs. Creates presumption.
Affirmative Defenses:	Defect does not substantially impair use, value, or safety of vehicle, or results from abuse, neglect, or unauthorized modifications or alterations.
Available Remedy:	Replacement or repurchase. Consumer may choose repurchase.
Refund Details:	Full purchase price, including sales tax, registration fees, and other incidental costs. Deduction for use before first report of defect.
Other Remedies:	Court may award costs and reasonable attorney's fees to consumer. May award reasonable fees to defendant if action frivolous or in bad faith. No limit on other consumer remedies. Violation is unlawful trade practice.
Arbitration:	If manufacturer maintains state-approved informal settlement procedure, consumer must use before entitled to refund or replacement.
Resale of Lemon:	No disclosure required.

District of Columbia—D.C. Stat. § 50-501 et seq.	
Vehicles Covered:	Passenger vehicle sold or registered in D.C. Excludes buses sold for public transportation, motorcycles, motor homes, and motorized recreational vehicles.
Persons Covered:	Purchaser or lessee, transferee during express warranty term, or any person entitled to enforce warranty.
Use Covered:	Vehicle designed for primary purpose of transporting driver and one or more passengers on streets, roads, or highways.
Defects Covered:	Defect that renders vehicle unreliable or unsafe for normal operation, or reduces its resale value below average resale value for comparable vehicles.
Period Covered:	Two years or 18,000 miles, whichever is first.
Notice Requirement:	Report defect to manufacturer or its agents within period covered.
"Reasonable" Repair Guidelines:	Either at least four repairs to same defect after notice within period covered, or at least one repair to safety-related defect after notice within period covered, or at least 30 days out of service for repairs within period covered. Creates presumption.
Affirmative Defenses:	Defect does not significantly impair operation, safety, performance, or value of vehicle, or results from abuse, neglect, or unauthorized modifications or alterations. Statute of limitations: four years from delivery.
Available Remedy:	Replacement or refund, at consumer's option.
Refund Details:	Full purchase price, including sales tax, license and registration fees, and similar government charges. Deduction for use after first 12,000 miles.
Other Remedies:	No limit on other consumer remedies. Violation is unlawful trade practice.
Arbitration:	Consumer must use government-run arbitration board procedure before filing suit.
Resale of Lemon:	Disclosure required; title branded.

Florida—Fla. Stat. § 681.10 et seq.	
Vehicles Covered:	New motor vehicles sold or leased in state to transport persons or property. Includes recreational vehicles and demonstrators. Excludes muscle-propelled vehicles, off-road vehicles, trucks over 10,000 pounds, motorcycles, mopeds, and living facilities of recreational vehicles.
Persons Covered:	Purchaser, lessee, transferee during period covered, or any person entitled to enforce warranty.
Use Covered:	Vehicle primarily used for personal, family, or household purposes.
Defects Covered:	Defect that substantially impairs use, value, or safety of vehicle.
Period Covered:	Two years.
Notice Requirement:	After three repairs to same defect or 15 calendar days out of service for repairs, written notice to manufacturer, by registered or express mail, of need to repair. Manufacturer entitled to final repair attempt after notice.
"Reasonable" Repair Guidelines:	Either at least three repairs to same defect, plus one final attempt after notice, or at least 30 days out of service for repairs (60 days for recreational vehicles). Creates presumption.
Affirmative Defenses:	Defect does not substantially impair use, value, or safety of vehicle, or results from accident abuse, neglect, or unauthorized modifications or alterations, or claim not filed in good faith. Statute of limitations: one year after period covered, or after settlement process or arbitration.
Available Remedy:	Replacement or refund. Consumer may choose refund.
Refund Details:	Cash price, including allowance for trade-in vehicle; collateral charges resulting from purchase or lease, such as sales tax, title charges, service charges, options, and earned finance charges; incidental costs resulting from defects. Deduction for use before settlement or arbitration hearing.
Other Remedies:	Possible additional damages of $25 per day; possible double or treble arbitration award. Mandatory litigation costs and reasonable attorney's fees to consumer. Mandatory costs and reasonable attorney's fees to manufacturer if consumer's claim frivolous or in bad faith. No limit on other consumer remedies. Violation is unfair trade practice.
Arbitration:	If manufacturer maintains informal settlement procedure, must notify consumer at time of sale, and consumer must use before entitled to replacement or refund. Consumer must also use state-run arbitration board before filing suit (after using manufacturer's procedure, if one exists). Special mediation/arbitration programs for recreational vehicles.
Resale of Lemon:	Disclosure required; one-year/12,000-mile warranty.

Georgia—Ga. Code § 10-1-780 et seq.	
Vehicles Covered:	New, self-propelled vehicles, purchased, leased, or originally registered in state, primarily designed for transportation of persons or property over public highways. Includes demonstrators and vehicles purchased at end of lease. Excludes living portion of motor homes, motorcycles, and trucks weighing 10,000 pounds or more.
Persons Covered:	Person with contract for transfer, lease, or purchase of new vehicle, or subsequent transferee; or business with ten or fewer employees, net yearly income of $100,000 or less, and three or fewer vehicles.
Use Covered:	Vehicle acquired primarily for personal, family, or household purposes.
Defects Covered:	Defect that makes vehicle unreliable or unsafe for ordinary use, or diminishes its resale value a meaningful amount below average resale value for comparable vehicles.
Period Covered:	First repair attempt must occur within one year or 12,000 miles, whichever is first. If first repair attempt occurs less than 15 days before end of period covered, period is extended 90 days.
Notice Requirement:	Written notice to manufacturer, by certified mail or overnight delivery, that vehicle not repaired after reasonable number of attempts. Manufacturer entitled to final repair attempt after notice.
"Reasonable" Repair Guidelines:	Within period covered, at least one repair to serious safety defect in brakes or steering. Alternately, within any period of two years or 24,000 miles, whichever is first: at least two repairs to other serious safety defect; or at least three repairs to any defect; or at least 30 calendar days out of service for repairs, 15 of which were within period covered. Creates presumption as matter of law.
Affirmative Defenses:	Defect does not substantially impair use, value, or safety of vehicle to consumer, or results from abuse, neglect, or unauthorized modifications or alterations.
Available Remedy:	Replacement or repurchase, at consumer's option.
Refund Details:	Cash price, including allowance for trade-in vehicle; collateral charges resulting from purchase or lease, such as sales tax, title charges, service charges, options, and finance charges; incidental expenses resulting from repairs, including repair costs, towing, and alternate transportation. Deduction for use before request for repurchase or replacement.
Other Remedies:	Court may award attorney's fees and costs to consumer. Consumer cannot seek both Commercial Code remedies for rejection or revocation of acceptance and lemon law remedies. No other limit on other consumer remedies. Violation or failure to honor warranty is unlawful trade practice.
Arbitration:	If manufacturer maintains informal settlement procedure, consumer must use before filing suit. Consumer must also use state-run arbitration before filing suit (after using manufacturer's procedure if one exists).
Resale of Lemon:	Disclosure required; one-year/12,000-mile warranty.

Hawaii—Haw. Rev. Stat. § 481I-1 et seq.	
Vehicles Covered:	New self-propelled vehicles primarily designed for transportation of persons or property over public streets and highways. Includes demonstrators; excludes mopeds, motorcycles, motor scooters, and vehicles over 10,000 pounds.
Persons Covered:	Purchaser, lessee, transferee during express warranty term, or any person entitled to enforce warranty.
Use Covered:	Vehicle used primarily for personal, family, or household purposes; or individual's business purposes and personal, family, or household purpose; or household, individual, or personal use and business use for business that has purchased or leased no more than one vehicle per year.
Defects Covered:	Defect that does not conform to express warranty and that renders vehicle unfit, unreliable, or unsafe, or significantly diminishes value of vehicle.
Period Covered:	Warranty term, two years, or 24,000 miles, whichever is first.
Notice Requirement:	Report defect in writing during period covered, but only if manufacturer provided written notice of terms of arbitration program and lemon law rights at time of purchase.
"Reasonable" Repair Guidelines:	Within period covered, either at least three repairs to same defect or at least one repair to serious safety defect, or at least 30 business days out of service for repairs. Creates presumption if manufacturer had written notice and opportunity to repair.
Affirmative Defenses:	Defect results from abuse, neglect, or unauthorized modifications or alterations by consumer. Statute of limitations: one year after period covered.
Available Remedy:	Replacement or refund.
Refund Details:	Cash price, including allowance for trade-in; collateral charges resulting from purchase or lease, such as excise tax, license and registration fees, preparation, transportation, options, and finance and interest charges; incidental expenses resulting from defects, including towing and alternate transportation. Excludes loss of use, loss of income, and personal injury. Deduction for use before third repair for same defect, first repair for serious safety defect, or 30th day out of service for repairs, whichever is first.
Other Remedies:	Mandatory costs and attorney's fees to prevailing party, whether consumer or manufacturer, if other party demands trial after arbitration but does not improve result. Failure to disclose resale of lemon is unfair or deceptive act or practice.
Arbitration:	Consumer may use state-run arbitration program.
Resale of Lemon:	Disclosure required; one-year/12,000-mile warranty.

Idaho—Idaho Code § 48-901 et seq.	
Vehicles Covered:	New motor vehicles, excluding motorcycles, farm tractors, trailers, and vehicles over 12,000 pounds.
Persons Covered:	Purchaser, lessee, or transferee during express warranty term.
Use Covered:	Vehicle used for personal business use, personal, family, or household purposes.
Defects Covered:	Defect that impairs use or market value of vehicle to consumer.
Period Covered:	Warranty term, two years, or 24,000 miles, whichever is first.
Notice Requirement:	Written notice to manufacturer or agents. Manufacturer entitled to at least one repair attempt.
"Reasonable" Repair Guidelines:	Within period covered, either at least four repairs to same defect, including at least one by manufacturer itself, or at least one repair to serious safety defect in brakes or steering, or at least 30 business days out of service for repairs. Creates presumption if above notice given. Repairs after period covered but within three years from delivery still count toward reasonable number of attempts if consumer originally reported defect during warranty term.
Affirmative Defenses:	Defect does not impair use or market value, or results from abuse, neglect, or unauthorized modifications or alterations. Statute of limitations: three years from delivery, or three months from decision of informal settlement mechanism.
Available Remedy:	Replacement or refund. Consumer may choose refund. If leased vehicle, refund only.
Refund Details:	Amount paid for vehicle, including options and value of trade-in; sales tax, license and registration fees, and charges resulting from repairs, including towing and rental expenses. Deduction for use before arbitration hearing.
Other Remedies:	Court may award reasonable attorney's fees to consumer, excluding fees incurred in connection with settlement mechanism. Mandatory treble damages, costs, and attorney's fees to prevailing party, whether consumer or manufacturer, if other party's demand for trial after settlement mechanism is in bad faith or frivolous. No limit on other consumer remedies. Violation also violates state Consumer Protection Act.
Arbitration:	Manufacturer must maintain informal settlement mechanism. Consumer must use mechanism before entitled to replacement or refund.
Resale of Lemon:	Disclosure required; one-year/12,000-mile warranty.

Illinois—815 Ill. Comp. Stat. § 380/1 et seq.	
Vehicles Covered:	New, self-propelled passenger cars designed for carrying not more than ten persons; new, self-propelled motor vehicles designed for carrying more than ten persons or for pulling or carrying freight or cargo, or designed or used for living quarters, that weigh less than 8,000 pounds; and new recreational vehicles, except camping trailers or travel trailers.
Persons Covered:	Individual purchaser or lessee.
Use Covered:	Vehicle purchased or leased for primarily personal, household, or family purposes.
Defects Covered:	Defect that does not conform to express warranty, and that substantially impairs use, market value, or safety of vehicle.
Period Covered:	One year or 12,000 miles, whichever is first.
Notice Requirement:	Direct written notice to manufacturer. Manufacturer entitled to at least one repair attempt. If no notice, no presumption of reasonable number of repair attempts.
"Reasonable" Repair Guidelines:	Within period covered, either at least four repairs to same defect or at least 30 business days out of service for repairs. Creates presumption if above notice given.
Affirmative Defenses:	Defect results from abuse, neglect, or unauthorized modifications or alterations. Statute of limitations: 18 months from delivery, extended while using informal settlement procedure.
Available Remedy:	Replacement or refund.
Refund Details:	Full purchase price or lease cost, including all collateral charges, but excluding taxes. Deduction for use before first report of defect, and for all subsequent time when vehicle is not being repaired.
Other Remedies:	Consumers seeking remedies under lemon law may not proceed under Commercial Code.
Arbitration:	If manufacturer maintains informal settlement procedure and gives consumer written notice, consumer must use before entitled to replacement or refund.
Resale of Lemon:	No disclosure required.

Note: Legislation is currently pending in Illinois legislature that, if passed, would substantially modify lemon law, effective January 1, 2005.

Indiana—Ind. Code § 24-5-13-1 et seq.	
Vehicles Covered:	Self-propelled motor vehicles sold, leased, transferred, or replaced in state, weighing less than 10,000 pounds. Excludes conversion vans, motor homes, farm tractors and other farm machines, road building equipment, truck tractors, road tractors, motorcycles, mopeds, snowmobiles, and off-road vehicles.
Persons Covered:	Person with contract for transfer, lease, or purchase of vehicle.
Use Covered:	Vehicle intended primarily for use and operation on public highways.
Defects Covered:	Defect that substantially impairs use, market value, or safety of vehicle, or does not conform to manufacturer's warranty.
Period Covered:	18 months or 18,000 miles, whichever is first.
Notice Requirement:	Direct notice to manufacturer of claim, but only if manufacturer discloses in warranty or owner's manual that written notice is required for refund or replacement.
"Reasonable" Repair Guidelines:	Either at least four repairs to same defect or at least 30 business days out of service for repairs.
Affirmative Defenses:	Defect does not substantially impair use, value, or safety of vehicle, or results from consumer's abuse, neglect, or unauthorized modification or alteration. Statute of limitations: two years from first report of defect, extended while using informal settlement procedure.
Available Remedy:	Refund or replacement, at consumer's option.
Refund Details:	Full contract price, including allowance for trade-in, options, sales tax, unexpended portion of registration fee, and finance charges expended; towing and rental costs actually incurred because of defect. Deduction for use before manufacturer's acceptance of return of vehicle.
Other Remedies:	Mandatory costs, expenses, and attorney's fees to consumer. No limit on other consumer remedies.
Arbitration:	If manufacturer maintains informal settlement procedure and gives consumer written notice, consumer must use before entitled to replacement or refund.
Resale of Lemon:	Disclosure required; one-year/12,000-mile warranty.

Iowa—Iowa Code § 322G.1 et seq.	
Vehicles Covered:	Self-propelled vehicles purchased or leased in state, or in other state if consumer is resident of Iowa when asserting rights. Excludes mopeds, motorcycles, motor homes, and vehicles over 10,000 pounds.
Persons Covered:	Purchaser or lessee of new vehicle, or any person entitled to enforce warranty during period covered.
Use Covered:	Vehicle primarily designed for transportation of persons or property over public streets and highways.
Defects Covered:	Defect that does not conform to warranty, and that renders vehicle unfit, unreliable, or unsafe, or significantly diminishes value of vehicle.
Period Covered:	Warranty term, two years, or 24,000 miles, whichever is first.
Notice Requirement:	After three repairs for same defect, or one repair for serious safety defect, or 20 days out of service for repairs, written notice to manufacturer by certified, registered, or overnight mail, of need to repair defect. Manufacturer entitled to final repair attempt after notice.
"Reasonable" Repair Guidelines:	During period covered, either at least three repairs to same defect, plus one final attempt by manufacturer; or at least one repair to serious safety defect, plus one final attempt by manufacturer; or at least 30 calendar days out of service for repairs. Creates presumption.
Affirmative Defenses:	Defect does not substantially impair vehicle, or results from accident, abuse, neglect, or unauthorized modification or alteration; claim not filed in good faith. Statute of limitations: one year from period covered.
Available Remedy:	Replacement or refund. Consumer may choose refund.
Refund Details:	Cash price paid for vehicle, including allowance for trade-in; collateral charges resulting from purchase or lease, such as use taxes, title charges, options, and finance charges; incidental expenses resulting from defects, including towing and alternate transportation. Excludes loss of use, loss of income, and personal injury. Deduction for use before third repair for same defect, first repair for serious safety defect, or 20th day out of service for repairs, whichever is first.
Other Remedies:	Possible additional damages of $25 per day; possible double or treble arbitration award. Court may award reasonable attorney's fees and costs to consumer. No limit on other consumer remedies. Violation is unfair trade practice.
Arbitration:	If manufacturer maintains informal settlement procedure, must give consumer written notice at time of purchase or lease, and consumer must use before entitled to replacement or refund.
Resale of Lemon:	Disclosure required; title branded.

Kansas—Kan. Stat. § 50-645	
Vehicles Covered:	New self-propelled motor vehicles sold or leased in state, less than 12,000 pounds. Excludes customized parts of vehicles added or modified by second stage manufacturers or converters.
Persons Covered:	Original purchaser or lessee.
Use Covered:	Any.
Defects Covered:	Defect that substantially impairs use or value of vehicle to consumer.
Period Covered:	Warranty term or one year, whichever is first.
Notice Requirement:	Actual notice to manufacturer. If no notice, no presumption of reasonable number of repair attempts.
"Reasonable" Repair Guidelines:	During period covered, either at least four repairs to same defect or at least 30 calendar days out of service for repairs. Alternately, at least 10 repairs for defects that substantially impair vehicle, even if beyond period covered. Creates presumption if above notice given.
Affirmative Defenses:	Defect does not significantly impair use or value, or results from abuse, neglect, or unauthorized modifications or alterations by consumer.
Available Remedy:	Replacement or refund.
Refund Details:	Full purchase or lease price, including all collateral charges. Deduction for use before first report of defect—including any use by prior owner—and for all subsequent time when vehicle is not being repaired.
Other Remedies:	No limit on other consumer remedies.
Arbitration:	If manufacturer maintains informal settlement procedure, must give consumer written notice at time of purchase or lease, and consumer must use before entitled to replacement or refund.
Resale of Lemon:	No disclosure required.

Kentucky—Ky. Rev. Stat. § 367.840 et seq.	
Vehicles Covered:	New self-propelled vehicles. Excludes vehicles substantially altered after sale, motor homes, motorcycles, mopeds, farm tractors and other farm machines, and vehicles with more than two axles.
Persons Covered:	Resident who buys, contracts to buy, or leases new vehicle in state.
Use Covered:	Vehicle intended primarily for use and operation on public highways.
Defects Covered:	Failure to conform with express warranty in manner that substantially impairs use, value, or safety of vehicle.
Period Covered:	One year or 12,000 miles, whichever is first.
Notice Requirement:	Report defect to manufacturer in writing during period covered.
"Reasonable" Repair Guidelines:	During period covered, either at least four repairs to same defect or at least 30 calendar days out of service for repairs. Creates presumption.
Affirmative Defenses:	Defect does not significantly impair use, value, or safety of vehicle, or results from abuse, neglect, or unauthorized modification or alteration by consumer. Statute of limitations: two years from delivery.
Available Remedy:	Replacement or refund, at consumer's option.
Refund Details:	Full purchase price, including finance charges, sales tax, license and registration fees, other government charges and collateral charges. Deduction for consumer's use when vehicle not out of service due to defect.
Other Remedies:	Court may award reasonable attorney's fees to consumer. No limit on other consumer remedies. Violation is unfair business practice.
Arbitration:	If manufacturer maintains dispute resolution system, consumer must use before filing suit.
Resale of Lemon:	No disclosure required.

Louisiana—La. Rev. Stat. § 51:1941 et seq.	
Vehicles Covered:	Passenger vehicles and passenger-and-commercial vehicles sold in state. Includes personal watercraft, all-terrain vehicles, and motor home chassis sold in state, if used exclusively for personal and not commercial purposes. Excludes vehicles other than motor homes over 10,000 pounds.
Persons Covered:	Purchaser, lessee, transferee during express warranty term, or any person entitled to enforce warranty.
Use Covered:	Vehicle not used exclusively for commercial purposes.
Defects Covered:	Defect that substantially impairs use, market value, or both of vehicle.
Period Covered:	Warranty term or one year, whichever is first.
Notice Requirement:	For motor homes, written notice to manufacturer of need for repair, at least 90 days out of service for repairs, and at least four repair attempts within period covered. Manufacturer entitled to final repair attempt after notice.
"Reasonable" Repair Guidelines:	During period covered, either at least four repairs to same defect or at least 90 calendar days out of service for repairs. Creates presumption, and imposes obligation on manufacturer to replace or refund.
Affirmative Defenses:	Statute of limitations: three years from purchase or one year from end of warranty term, whichever is first.
Available Remedy:	Replacement or refund, at manufacturer's option.
Refund Details:	Full purchase price, including all amounts paid at time of sale; sales tax, license and registration fees, and similar government charges. Deduction for use before first report of defect, and for all subsequent time when vehicle is not being repaired.
Other Remedies:	Mandatory reasonable attorney's fees actually incurred. No limit on other consumer remedies.
Arbitration:	If manufacturer maintains informal settlement procedure, consumer must use before entitled to replacement or refund.
Resale of Lemon:	Disclosure required; title branded.

Maine—10 Me. Rev. Stat. § 1161 et seq.	
Vehicles Covered:	Vehicles sold or leased in state. Excludes vehicles over 8,500 pounds used primarily for commercial purposes.
Persons Covered:	Purchaser or lessee, transferees during express warranty term, or any person entitled to enforce warranty. Excludes government entity, business or commercial entity with at least three vehicles.
Use Covered:	Vehicle designed for conveyance of passengers or property on public highways.
Defects Covered:	Defect or combination of defects that substantially impairs use, value, or safety of vehicle.
Period Covered:	Warranty term, three years, or 18,000 miles, whichever is first.
Notice Requirement:	Written notice to manufacturer or authorized dealer of consumer's desire for refund or replacement, but only if manufacturer discloses in warranty or owner's manual that written notice is required for refund or replacement. Manufacturer entitled to final repair attempt after notice.
"Reasonable" Repair Guidelines:	During period covered, either at least three repairs to same defect, at least one repair to serious braking or steering defect, or at least 15 business days out of service for repairs. Creates presumption.
Affirmative Defenses:	Defect does not substantially impair use, value, or safety of vehicle, or results from abuse, neglect, or unauthorized modifications or alterations.
Available Remedy:	Replacement or refund. Consumer may reject replacement and choose refund.
Refund Details:	Full purchase price, including paid finance charges; sales tax, license and registration fees, and other collateral charges; reasonable costs incurred for towing, storage, and alternate transportation. Deduction for use before application to arbitration procedure plus all mileage over 20,000, but not to exceed 10% of purchase price.
Other Remedies:	Court may award reasonable attorney's fees and costs to consumer. Possible additional damages of $25 per day; possible double arbitration award. No limit on other consumer remedies. Violation is unfair trade practice.
Arbitration:	If manufacturer maintains informal settlement procedure, consumer must use before entitled to replacement or refund. Consumer may also request state-certified arbitration.
Resale of Lemon:	Disclosure required.

Maryland—Md. Comm. L. Code § 14-1501	
Vehicles Covered:	Passenger vehicles, motorcycles, trucks that are ¾-ton or less, and multi-purpose vehicles, registered in state. Excludes motor homes and fleet purchases of five or more vehicles.
Persons Covered:	Purchaser, transferee during express warranty term, or any person entitled to enforce warranty.
Use Covered:	Any.
Defects Covered:	Defect that substantially impairs use and market value of vehicle to consumer.
Period Covered:	15 months or 15,000 miles, whichever is first.
Notice Requirement:	Written notice of defect to manufacturer or agent by certified mail during period covered.
"Reasonable" Repair Guidelines:	During period covered, either at least four repairs to same defect; or at least one repair to serious braking or steering defect, plus additional opportunity to cure after notice; or at least 30 days out of service for repairs. Creates presumption.
Affirmative Defenses:	Defect does not significantly substantially impair use and market value of vehicle, or results from abuse, neglect, or unauthorized modifications or alterations.
Available Remedy:	Replacement or refund, at consumer's option.
Refund Details:	Full purchase price, including license and registration fees and similar government charges. Deduction for all use, not to exceed 15% of purchase price.
Other Remedies:	Possible penalty up to $10,000 for bad faith violation. Court may award reasonable attorney's fees to plaintiff. Court may award reasonable attorney's fees to other party if action frivolous or in bad faith. No limit on other consumer remedies. Violation is unfair and deceptive trade practice.
Arbitration:	If manufacturer maintains informal settlement procedure, consumer may use before seeking replacement or refund.
Resale of Lemon:	Disclosure required.

Massachusetts—Mass. Gen. L. ch. 90, § 7N½	
Vehicles Covered:	Motor vehicles sold, leased, or replaced by dealer or manufacturer. Includes motorcycles. Excludes auto homes and off-road vehicles.
Persons Covered:	Buyer, lessee, transferee during express warranty term, or any person entitled to enforce warranty.
Use Covered:	Vehicle not used primarily for business purposes.
Defects Covered:	Defect or combination of defects that substantially impairs use, market value, or safety of vehicle.
Period Covered:	One year or 15,000 miles, whichever is first.
Notice Requirement:	None required before arbitration.
"Reasonable" Repair Guidelines:	During period covered, either at least three repairs to same defect or at least 15 business days out of service for repairs, plus one final opportunity to cure. Repair attempts deemed reasonable.
Affirmative Defenses:	Defect does not substantially impair use, market value, or safety of vehicle, or results from consumer's negligence, accident, vandalism, unauthorized repair attempt, or unauthorized substantial modification. Statute of limitations: consumer must request arbitration within 18 months.
Available Remedy:	Refund or replacement. Consumer may reject replacement and demand refund.
Refund Details:	Full purchase price, including allowance for trade-in; incidental costs, including sales tax, registration fees, finance charges, and options; towing and reasonable rental costs. Deduction for use before manufacturer accepts return of vehicle.
Other Remedies:	Possible additional damages of $25 per day; possible double arbitration award. Mandatory reasonable attorney's fees and costs to consumer on manufacturer's appeal from arbitration. No limit on other consumer remedies. Violation is unfair or deceptive act.
Arbitration:	If consumer requests, manufacturer must submit to state-certified arbitration.
Resale of Lemon:	Disclosure required.

Michigan—Mich. Comp. Laws § 257.1401 et seq.

Vehicles Covered:	Passenger or sport utility vehicles purchased or leased in state or by a resident of state. Includes pickup trucks and vans. Excludes other trucks, motor homes, or vehicles with less than four wheels.
Persons Covered:	Individual, business, or other legal entity that purchases or leases less than 10 vehicles per year, or that purchases or leases 10 or more vehicles per year for personal, family, or household purposes; or any other person entitled to enforce warranty.
Use Covered:	Any, but if consumer purchases or leases 10 or more vehicles per year, then vehicle must be purchased or leased for personal, family, or household use and not for resale.
Defects Covered:	Defect that impairs use or value of vehicle to consumer, or prevents vehicle from conforming to warranty.
Period Covered:	Warranty term or one year, whichever is first.
Notice Requirement:	Written notice to manufacturer of need for repair, by return receipt service, after third repair attempt or at least 25 days out of service for repairs. Manufacturer entitled to final repair attempt after notice.
"Reasonable" Repair Guidelines:	Either at least four repairs to same defect, within two years from first attempt, or at least 30 days out of service for repairs during covered period. Creates presumption.
Affirmative Defenses:	Defect results from unauthorized modification, abuse, neglect, or accident.
Available Remedy:	Replacement or refund. Consumer may demand refund.
Refund Details:	Purchase price, including allowance for trade-in, but excluding any negative equity, discount, rebate, or incentive; sales tax, license and registration fees, and similar government charges; options and modifications; towing and rental costs reasonably incurred. Deduction for use before first report of defect—including any use by prior owner—plus all mileage beyond 25,000, less any period during which vehicle did not provide useful transportation.
Other Remedies:	Court may award costs, expenses, and attorney's fees to consumer. No limit on other consumer remedies.
Arbitration:	If manufacturer maintains informal settlement procedure, consumer must use before entitled to replacement or refund.
Resale of Lemon:	No disclosure required.

Minnesota—Minn. Stat. § 325F.665	
Vehicles Covered:	Passenger automobiles, including pickup trucks and vans, sold or leased in state. Includes chassis or van portion of recreational vehicles.
Persons Covered:	Purchaser, lessee, or transferee during express warranty term.
Use Covered:	Vehicle used for personal, family, or household purposes at least 40% of the time.
Defects Covered:	Defect that substantially impairs use or market value of vehicle to consumer.
Period Covered:	Warranty term or two years, whichever is first.
Notice Requirement:	Written notice to manufacturer or agent, and opportunity to cure. If no notice and opportunity to cure, no presumption of reasonable number of repair attempts.
"Reasonable" Repair Guidelines:	During period covered—or within thee years if first reported within warranty term—either at least four repairs to same defect or at least one repair to serious braking or steering failure, or at least 30 business days out of service for repairs. Creates presumption if above notice given.
Affirmative Defenses:	Defect does not substantially impair use or market value of vehicle, or results from abuse, neglect, or unauthorized modifications or alterations. Statute of limitations: three years from delivery, or six months from decision of informal settlement mechanism.
Available Remedy:	Replacement or refund. Consumer may reject replacement and require refund. If lease, refund only, no replacement.
Refund Details:	Purchase price, including allowance for trade-in, options, and authorized modifications; all other charges, including prorated sales or excise tax, license and registration fees; towing and rental expenses. Deduction for use by consumer—and any previous consumer—when use and market value of vehicle not substantially impaired.
Other Remedies:	Court may award costs, disbursements, and reasonable attorney's fees to consumer. Possible treble damages, costs and disbursements, and reasonable attorney's fees to prevailing party, whether consumer or manufacturer, if appeal of arbitration decision is frivolous or in bad faith. No limit on other consumer remedies.
Arbitration:	Manufacturer must maintain informal settlement mechanism, and consumer must use before entitled to replacement or refund.
Resale of Lemon:	Disclosure required; 12-month/12,000-mile warranty.

Mississippi—Miss. Code § 63-17-151 et seq.	
Vehicles Covered:	Vehicles sold in state, not propelled by muscular power, operated over public streets and highways, used to transport persons or property. Includes demonstrators and lease-purchases. Excludes vehicles run only on tracks, off-road vehicles, motorcycles, mopeds, electric personal assistive mobility devices, and parts and components of motor homes added on or assembled by manufacturer.
Persons Covered:	Purchaser, transferee during express warranty term, or any person entitled to enforce warranty.
Use Covered:	Defect impairs use, market value, or safety of vehicle to consumer.
Defects Covered:	Vehicle used primarily for personal, family, or household purposes.
Period Covered:	Warranty term or one year, whichever is first.
Notice Requirement:	Written notice of need for repair. Manufacturer entitled to final repair attempt after notice.
"Reasonable" Repair Guidelines:	During period covered, either at least three repairs to same defect or at least 15 working days out of service for repairs. Creates presumption.
Affirmative Defenses:	Defect does not impair use, market value, or safety of vehicle, or results from consumer's abuse, neglect, or unauthorized modifications or alterations; claim not filed in good faith. Statute of limitations: 18 months from delivery or one year from end of warranty term, whichever is first, or 90 days from final action of informal settlement panel.
Available Remedy:	Replacement or refund, at consumer's option.
Refund Details:	Full purchase price; collateral charges, including title, transportation, and dealer preparation charges, and towing and rental costs. Deduction for all use by consumer.
Other Remedies:	Court may award costs, expenses, and attorney's fees. Mandatory court costs to manufacturer if claim filed in bad faith. No limit on other consumer remedies.
Arbitration:	If manufacturer maintains informal settlement procedure and notifies consumer, consumer must use before entitled to replacement or refund.
Resale of Lemon:	No disclosure required.

Missouri—Mo. Rev. Stat. § 407.560 et seq.	
Vehicles Covered:	New vehicles not propelled by muscular power. Includes lease-purchases, demonstrators, and chassis portion of recreational vehicles. Excludes commercial vehicles, off-road vehicles, mopeds, motorcycles, and other parts of recreational vehicles.
Persons Covered:	Purchaser, transferee during express warranty term, or any person entitled to enforce warranty.
Use Covered:	Vehicle primarily used for personal, family, or household purposes.
Defects Covered:	Defect impairs use, market value, or safety of vehicle to consumer.
Period Covered:	Warranty term or one year, whichever is first.
Notice Requirement:	Written notice to manufacturer of need for repair. Manufacturer entitled to final repair attempt after notice.
"Reasonable" Repair Guidelines:	During period covered, either at least four repairs to same defect or at least 30 working days out of service for repairs. Creates presumption.
Affirmative Defenses:	Defect does not substantially impair use, market value, or safety of vehicle, or results from abuse, neglect, or unauthorized modifications or alterations; claim not filed in good faith. Statute of limitations: 18 months from delivery or six months from end of warranty term, whichever is first, or 90 days from final action of informal settlement panel.
Available Remedy:	Replacement or refund, at manufacturer's option.
Refund Details:	Full purchase price, including collateral charges such as sales tax, title fees, license and registration fees. Deduction for use.
Other Remedies:	Mandatory costs, expenses, and attorney's fees to consumer. Mandatory costs and reasonable attorney's fees to manufacturer if claim filed in bad faith or consumer's recovery not at least 10% greater than manufacturer's offer. Commercial Code does not apply to new motor vehicle sales. No other limit on other consumer remedies.
Arbitration:	If manufacturer maintains informal settlement procedure, consumer must use before entitled to replacement or refund.
Resale of Lemon:	No disclosure required.

Montana—Mont. Code § 61-4-501 et seq.	
Vehicles Covered:	Self-propelled vehicles sold or registered in state. Includes non-residential portion of motor homes. Excludes trucks over 10,000 pounds, and components and systems of motor homes primarily for residential purposes.
Persons Covered:	Purchaser, transferee during express warranty term, or any person entitled to enforce warranty.
Use Covered:	Vehicle designed primarily to transport persons or property upon public highways.
Defects Covered:	Defect substantially impairs use and market value or safety of vehicle to consumer.
Period Covered:	Two years or 18,000 miles, whichever is first.
Notice Requirement:	Consumer may give written notice of defect to manufacturer or agent.
"Reasonable" Repair Guidelines:	Either at least four repairs to same defect during warranty period, or at least 30 business days out of service for repairs during warranty period after notice of defect. Creates presumption.
Affirmative Defenses:	Defect does not substantially impair use, market value, or safety of vehicle, or results from abuse, neglect, or unauthorized modification or alteration by consumer.
Available Remedy:	Replacement or refund, at manufacturer's option.
Refund Details:	Full purchase price; collateral charges, including sales tax, property tax, license and registration fees; incidental and consequential damages. Deduction for use before first written notice of defect, and for all subsequent time when vehicle is not out of service due to defect.
Other Remedies:	No limit on other consumer remedies. Violation is unfair or deceptive trade practice.
Arbitration:	If manufacturer maintains informal settlement procedure, consumer must use before entitled to replacement or refund.
Resale of Lemon:	Disclosure required.

Nebraska—Neb. Rev. Stat. § 60-2701 et seq.	
Vehicles Covered:	New motor vehicles sold in state. Excludes trailers and self-propelled mobile homes.
Persons Covered:	Purchaser, transferee during express warranty term, or any person entitled to enforce warranty.
Use Covered:	Vehicle normally used for personal, family, household, or business purposes.
Defects Covered:	Defect that substantially impairs use and market value of vehicle to consumer.
Period Covered:	Warranty term or one year, whichever is first.
Notice Requirement:	Written notice directly to manufacturer by certified mail, and opportunity to cure defect. If no notice and opportunity to cure, no presumption of reasonable number of repair attempts.
"Reasonable" Repair Guidelines:	During period covered, either at least four repairs to same defect or at least 40 days out of service for repairs. Creates presumption if above notice given.
Affirmative Defenses:	Defect does not significantly impair use and market value of vehicle to consumer, or results from consumer's abuse, neglect, or unauthorized modifications or alterations. Statute of limitations: two years from delivery or one year from end of warranty term, whichever is first.
Available Remedy:	Replacement or refund.
Refund Details:	Full purchase price, including sales tax, license and registration fees, and similar government charges. Deduction for use before first report of defect—including any use by prior owner—and for all subsequent time when vehicle is not being repaired.
Other Remedies:	Mandatory reasonable attorney's fees to consumer. No limit on other consumer remedies.
Arbitration:	If manufacturer maintains informal settlement procedure, consumer must use before entitled to replacement or refund.
Resale of Lemon:	No disclosure required.

Nevada—Nev. Rev. Stat. § 597.600 et seq.

Vehicles Covered:	Self-propelled vehicles by which person or property may be transported on public highways. Excludes vehicles moved by human power, vehicles used exclusively on rails or tracks, electric personal assistive mobility devices, motor homes, and off-road vehicles.
Persons Covered:	Person who purchases or contracts to purchase vehicle, transferee during express warranty term, or any person entitled to enforce warranty.
Use Covered:	Vehicle normally used for personal, family, or household purposes.
Defects Covered:	Defect that substantially impairs use and value of vehicle to buyer, and does not result from abuse, neglect, or unauthorized modifications or alterations.
Period Covered:	Warranty term or one year, whichever is first.
Notice Requirement:	None specified.
"Reasonable" Repair Guidelines:	During period covered, either at least four repairs to same defect or at least 30 calendar days out of service for repairs. Creates presumption.
Affirmative Defenses:	Statute of limitations: 18 months from delivery.
Available Remedy:	Replacement or refund.
Refund Details:	Full purchase price, including sales tax, license and registration fees, and similar government charges. Deduction for use before first report of defect, and for all subsequent time when vehicle is not being repaired.
Other Remedies:	No limit on other consumer remedies.
Arbitration:	If manufacturer maintains informal settlement procedure, consumer must use before entitled to replacement or refund.
Resale of Lemon:	No disclosure required.

New Hampshire—N.H. Rev. Stat. § 357-D	
Vehicles Covered:	Private passenger vehicles, station wagons, and all other four-wheel motor vehicles. Includes mopeds, motorcycles, and off-highway recreational vehicles. Excludes vehicles over 9,000 pounds and tractors.
Persons Covered:	Purchaser, lessee for at least two years, transferee during express warranty term, or any person entitled to enforce warranty. Excludes government entities.
Use Covered:	Any, except for vehicle purchased for purposes of resale.
Defects Covered:	Defect that substantially impairs use, market value, or safety of vehicle to consumer.
Period Covered:	Warranty term.
Notice Requirement:	After third repair attempt or 30 business days out of service, written notice to manufacturer of defect, and election between manufacturer's dispute settlement mechanism and state-run arbitration. Manufacturer entitled to final repair attempt after notice.
"Reasonable" Repair Guidelines:	During warranty term, either at least three repairs to same defect or at least 30 business days out of service for repairs. Creates presumption.
Affirmative Defenses:	Defect does not substantially impair use, market value, or safety of vehicle, or results from abuse, neglect, or unauthorized modifications or alterations by consumer. Statute of limitations: one year from end of warranty term or from manufacturer's final repair attempt, whichever is later.
Available Remedy:	Replacement or refund, at consumer's option.
Refund Details:	Full purchase price, including allowance for trade-in; license and registration fees, finance charges, and similar charges; incidental and consequential damages. Deduction for use before first repair attempt.
Other Remedies:	Court may award costs and reasonable attorney's fees to consumer. Court may award costs and reasonable attorney's fees to manufacturer if action brought without substantial justification. Failure to comply with arbitration decision is unfair and deceptive act or practice. Remedies not available if consumer has discontinued payments for vehicle.
Arbitration:	Consumer must use either manufacturer's informal dispute settlement mechanism or state-run arbitration, at consumer's option.
Resale of Lemon:	No disclosure required, but manufacturer may not resell vehicle determined to have serious safety defect.

New Jersey—N.J. Stat. § 56:12-29 et seq.	
Vehicles Covered:	Passenger vehicles and motorcycles, not propelled by muscular power, purchased, leased, or registered in state. Excludes vehicles that run on tracks or rails, motorized bicycles, and living facilities of motor homes.
Persons Covered:	Purchaser, lessee, transferee during express warranty term, or any person entitled to enforce warranty.
Use Covered:	Any.
Defects Covered:	Defect that substantially impairs use, value, or safety of vehicle.
Period Covered:	18,000 miles or two years, whichever is first.
Notice Requirement:	After two repairs to same defect or 20 calendar days out of service for repairs, written notice of potential claim to manufacturer by certified mail, return receipt requested. Manufacturer entitled to final repair attempt after notice. If no notice and opportunity to cure, no presumption of reasonable number of repair attempts.
"Reasonable" Repair Guidelines:	During period covered, either at least three repairs to same defect or at least 20 calendar days out of service for repairs. Creates presumption if above notice given.
Affirmative Defenses:	Defect does not substantially impair use, value, or safety of vehicle, or results from abuse, neglect, or unauthorized modifications or alterations.
Available Remedy:	Refund. Manufacturer may offer replacement instead, but consumer may reject and demand refund.
Refund Details:	Purchase price, including allowance for trade-in, options, sales tax, license and registration fees, finance charges, towing, rental expenses actually incurred, and other charges or fees. Deduction for use before first repair attempt.
Other Remedies:	Mandatory reasonable attorney's fees, expert fees, and court costs to consumer. Possible mandatory treble damages on manufacturer's frivolous appeal from state-run arbitration decision. No limit on other consumer remedies.
Arbitration:	Consumer may choose to use state-run arbitration, or manufacturer's informal settlement procedure if manufacturer maintains one.
Resale of Lemon:	Disclosure required.

New Mexico—N.M. Stat. § 57-16A-1 et seq.

Vehicles Covered:	New passenger motor vehicles, less than 10,000 pounds, sold and registered in state. Includes automobiles, pickup trucks, motorcycles, and vans.
Persons Covered:	Purchaser, transferee during express warranty term, or any persons entitled to enforce warranty.
Use Covered:	Vehicle normally used for personal, family, or household purposes.
Defects Covered:	Defect that substantially impairs use and market value of vehicle to consumer.
Period Covered:	Warranty term or one year, whichever is first.
Notice Requirement:	Direct written notice to manufacturer. Manufacturer entitled to final repair attempt after notice. If no notice and opportunity to cure, no presumption of reasonable number of repair attempts.
"Reasonable" Repair Guidelines:	During period covered, either at least four repairs to same defect or at least 30 business days out of service for repairs. Creates presumption if above notice given.
Affirmative Defenses:	Defect does not substantially impair use and market value of vehicle, or results from abuse, neglect, or unauthorized modifications or alterations; claim not filed in good faith. Statute of limitations: 18 months from delivery or 90 days from final action of informal settlement panel, whichever is later.
Available Remedy:	Replacement or refund.
Refund Details:	Full purchase price, including collateral charges such as taxes, license, title and registration fees, and other government charges. Deduction for use before first report of defect, and for all subsequent time when vehicle is not being repaired.
Other Remedies:	Mandatory reasonable attorney's fees and court costs to consumer. Mandatory reasonable attorney's fees and court costs to manufacturer if consumer's action frivolous or in bad faith. Consumers seeking remedies under lemon law may not proceed under Commercial Code.
Arbitration:	If manufacturer maintains informal settlement procedure, consumer must use before entitled to replacement or refund.
Resale of Lemon:	Disclosure required.

New York—N.Y. Cons. Laws, Gen. Bus. § 198-a et seq.

Vehicles Covered:	Motor vehicles purchased, leased, transferred, or registered in state. Excludes off-road vehicles, residential portion of motor homes, used vehicles with over 100,000 miles or sold for less than $1,500, and used motor homes. Excludes motorcycles until September 1, 2004.
Persons Covered:	Purchaser, lessee, transferee—if used vehicle, transferee if spouse or child of purchaser or lessee—or any person entitled to enforce warranty.
Use Covered:	Vehicle used primarily for personal, family, or household purposes.
Defects Covered:	Defect that substantially impairs value of vehicle to consumer.
Period Covered:	18,000 miles or two years, whichever is first.
Notice Requirement:	New vehicles only: Report defect to manufacturer or agent within period covered. If agent refuses repairs, written notice of refusal to manufacturer by certified mail, return receipt requested. Motor homes: After third repair for same defect or 21 days out of service for repairs, written notice to manufacturer or agent by certified mail, return receipt requested, but only if manufacturer has previously given consumer notice of this requirement. Further repairs to motor home do not count towards reasonable number of repair attempts until notice given.
"Reasonable" Repair Guidelines:	New vehicles: During period covered, either at least four repairs to same defect or at least 30 calendar days out of service for repairs. Used vehicles: During warranty period, either at least three repairs to same defect or at least 15 calendar days out of service for repairs. Creates presumption.
Affirmative Defenses:	Defect does not substantially impair value of vehicle to consumer, or results from abuse, neglect, or unauthorized modifications or alterations. Statute of limitations: four years from delivery.
Available Remedy:	Replacement or refund, at consumer's option.
Refund Details:	Purchase price, including allowance for trade-in; fees and charges, including sales tax, license and registration fees, and similar government charges. New vehicles: Deduction for use over 12,000 miles.
Other Remedies:	Court may award reasonable attorney's fees to consumer after arbitration. No limit on other consumer remedies.
Arbitration:	If manufacturer maintains informal settlement procedure, consumer must use before entitled to replacement or refund. Consumer may submit to state-run arbitration.
Resale of Lemon:	Disclosure required.

North Carolina—N.C. Gen. Stat. § 20-351 et seq.	
Vehicles Covered:	New self-propelled vehicles, and new vehicles designed to run on highways and pulled by self-propelled vehicles, sold or leased in state. Excludes mopeds, house trailers, and vehicles over 10,000 pounds.
Persons Covered:	Purchaser, lessee, or any person entitled to enforce warranty.
Use Covered:	Any.
Defects Covered:	Defect that substantially impairs value of vehicle to consumer.
Period Covered:	Two years or 24,000 miles.
Notice Requirement:	Direct written notice of defect to manufacturer and opportunity to cure, but only if manufacturer has previously given consumer notice of this requirement. If no notice when required, no presumption of reasonable number of repair attempts. Written notice of intent to sue ten days before filing a civil suit.
"Reasonable" Repair Guidelines:	Either at least four repairs to same defect or at least 20 business days out of service for repairs during any 12-month period. Creates presumption if above notice given.
Affirmative Defenses:	Defect results from abuse, neglect, odometer tampering by consumer, or unauthorized modifications or alterations.
Available Remedy:	Replacement or refund, at consumer's option.
Refund Details:	Full contract price, including charges for dealer preparation and transportation, options, and service contracts; collateral charges, including sales tax, license and registration fees, and similar government charges; finance charges after first report of defect; incidental and consequential damages. Deduction for use before first report of defect, and for all subsequent time when vehicle is not being repaired.
Other Remedies:	Injunctive or other equitable relief. Possible treble damages. Possible reasonable attorney's fees to prevailing party. No limit on other consumer remedies.
Arbitration:	If manufacturer maintains informal settlement procedure, manufacturer may require consumer to use before filing suit if manufacturer discloses that requirement to consumer.
Resale of Lemon:	Disclosure required.

North Dakota—N.D. Cent. Code § 51-07-16

Vehicles Covered:	Self-propelled vehicles, vehicles propelled by overhead electric wires and not operated on rails, motorized bicycles, and trucks not over 10,000 pounds, sold or leased in state. Excludes snowmobiles and house cars.
Persons Covered:	Purchaser, lessee, transferee during express warranty term, or any person entitled to enforce warranty.
Use Covered:	Vehicle normally used for personal, family, or household purposes.
Defects Covered:	Defect substantially impairs use and market value of vehicle.
Period Covered:	Warranty term or one year, whichever is first.
Notice Requirement:	Direct notice and opportunity to cure. If no notice, no presumption of reasonable number of repair attempts.
"Reasonable" Repair Guidelines:	During period covered, more than three repairs to same defect or at least 30 business days out of service for repairs. Creates presumption if above notice given.
Affirmative Defenses:	Defect does not substantially impair use and market value of vehicle, or results from abuse, neglect, or unauthorized modifications or alterations by consumer. Statute of limitations: six months after either end of warranty or 18 months from delivery, whichever is first.
Available Remedy:	Replacement or refund.
Refund Details:	Full purchase price, including all collateral charges. Deduction for use before first report of defect and for all subsequent time when vehicle is not being repaired, not to exceed 10% of purchase price.
Other Remedies:	Exclusive remedy; if consumer proceeds under lemon law, may not pursue any other remedies.
Arbitration:	If manufacturer maintains informal settlement procedure, consumer must use before entitled to replacement or refund.
Resale of Lemon:	Disclosure required; minimum 12-month/12,000-mile warranty.

Ohio—Ohio Rev. Code § 1345.71 et seq.	
Vehicles Covered:	Passenger cars, non-commercial vehicles, and portion of motor homes not used for storage, cooking, eating, or sleeping. Excludes motorized bicycles, construction equipment, farm equipment, boat trailers, mobile homes, recreational vehicles, and manufactured homes.
Persons Covered:	Purchaser, lessee for at least 30 days, transferee during express warranty term, or any person entitled to enforce warranty.
Use Covered:	Vehicle designed and used for carrying not more than 9 persons (or not more than 15 persons in a ridesharing arrangement), or used exclusively for purposes other than business for profit.
Defects Covered:	Defect substantially impairs use, value, or safety of vehicle to consumer and does not conform to warranty.
Period Covered:	One year or 18,000 miles, whichever is first.
Notice Requirement:	None.
"Reasonable" Repair Guidelines:	During period covered, at least three repairs to same defect, or at least eight repairs to any defect, or at least one repair to serious safety defect, or at least 30 calendar days out of service for repairs. Creates presumption.
Affirmative Defenses:	Defect results from abuse, neglect, or unauthorized modification or alteration. Statute of limitations: five years from delivery, extended while using informal dispute resolution procedure.
Available Remedy:	Replacement or refund, at consumer's option.
Refund Details:	Full purchase price, including charges for transportation, options and accessories, dealer preparation and delivery; finance charges, insurance, and service contract charges; sales tax, license and registration fees, and other government charges; incidental damages and expenses, including towing, rental, meals, and lodging. No deduction for use.
Other Remedies:	Mandatory award of reasonable attorney's fees and court costs to consumer. No limit on other consumer remedies. Violation is unfair and deceptive act or practice.
Arbitration:	If state establishes qualified informal dispute resolution procedure and notifies consumer, consumer must use before filing suit.
Resale of Lemon:	Disclosure required; 12-month/12,000-mile warranty; title branded.

Oklahoma—15 Okla. Stat. § 901	
Vehicles Covered:	New motor vehicles registered in state. Excludes vehicles over 10,000 pounds and living facilities of motor homes.
Persons Covered:	Purchasers, transferee during express warranty term, or any person entitled to enforce warranty.
Use Covered:	Any.
Defects Covered:	Defect that substantially impairs use and value of vehicle to consumer.
Period Covered:	Warranty term or one year, whichever is first.
Notice Requirement:	Direct written notice to manufacturer, and opportunity to cure. If no notice, no presumption of reasonable number of repair attempts.
"Reasonable" Repair Guidelines:	During period covered, at least four repairs to same defect or at least 45 calendar days out of service for repairs. Creates presumption if above notice given.
Affirmative Defenses:	Defect does not substantially impair use and value of vehicle, or results from consumer's abuse, neglect, or unauthorized modifications or alterations.
Available Remedy:	Replacement or refund.
Refund Details:	Full purchase price, including taxes, license and registration fees, and other government charges, but excluding interest. Deduction for use before first written report of defect, and for all subsequent time when vehicle is not being repaired.
Other Remedies:	No limit on other consumer remedies.
Arbitration:	If manufacturer maintains informal settlement procedure, consumer must use before entitled to replacement or refund.
Resale of Lemon:	No disclosure.

Oregon—Or. Rev. Stat. § 646.315 et seq.	
Vehicles Covered:	New self-propelled passenger motor vehicles sold in state.
Persons Covered:	Purchaser, lessee, transferee during express warranty term, or any person entitled to enforce warranty.
Use Covered:	Vehicle normally used for personal, family, or household purposes.
Defects Covered:	Defect that substantially impairs use, market value, or safety of vehicle to consumer.
Period Covered:	One year or 12,000 miles, whichever is first.
Notice Requirement:	Defect originally reported to manufacturer or agent within period covered; direct written notice to manufacturer, and opportunity to cure.
"Reasonable" Repair Guidelines:	During period covered, at least four repairs to same defect or at least 30 business days out of service for repairs. Creates presumption if above notice given.
Affirmative Defenses:	Defect does not substantially impair use, market value, or safety of vehicle, or results from abuse, neglect, or unauthorized modifications or alterations by consumer. Statute of limitations: one year from end of period covered.
Available Remedy:	Replacement or refund.
Refund Details:	Full purchase or lease price, including taxes, fees, and similar collateral charges, but excluding interest. Deduction for use before first report of defect, and for all subsequent time when vehicle is not being repaired.
Other Remedies:	Possible treble damages, maximum $50,000. No limit on other consumer remedies, but may not also obtain excess damages under lemon law.
Arbitration:	If manufacturer maintains informal settlement procedure, consumer must use before entitled to replacement or refund.
Resale of Lemon:	No disclosure.

Pennsylvania—73 P.S. § 1951 et seq.	
Vehicles Covered:	New and unused self-propelled, motorized vehicles, purchased and registered in state, driven on public roads, and designed to transport not more than 15 persons. Includes demonstrators and dealer cars. Excludes motorcycles, motor homes, and off-road vehicles.
Persons Covered:	Person who purchases or contracts to purchase new vehicle, transferee, successor, or assignee.
Use Covered:	Vehicle used or bought for use primarily for personal, family, or household purposes.
Defects Covered:	Defect that substantially impairs use, value, or safety of vehicle and does not conform to express warranty, and that does not result from abuse, neglect, or unauthorized modifications or alterations.
Period Covered:	One year or 12,000 miles, whichever is first.
Notice Requirement:	If consumer unable to deliver vehicle for repair, written notice to manufacturer.
"Reasonable" Repair Guidelines:	During period covered, at least three repairs to same defect or at least 30 calendar days out of service for repairs. Creates presumption.
Affirmative Defenses:	None specified.
Available Remedy:	Replacement or refund, at consumer's option.
Refund Details:	Full purchase price, including all collateral charges. Deduction for use before first report of defect to manufacturer, not to exceed 10% of purchase price.
Other Remedies:	Mandatory reasonable attorney's fees and court costs to consumer. No limit on other consumer remedies. Violation is unfair trade practices.
Arbitration:	If manufacturer maintains informal settlement procedure, consumer must use before entitled to replacement or refund.
Resale of Lemon:	Disclosure required; 12-month/12,000-mile warranty.

Rhode Island—R.I. Gen. Laws § 31-5.2-1 et seq.	
Vehicles Covered:	Automobiles, trucks, motorcycles, and vans less than 10,000 pounds. Excludes motorized campers.
Persons Covered:	Buyer, lessor, transferee during express or implied warranty term, or any person entitled to enforce warranty.
Use Covered:	Any.
Defects Covered:	Defect that substantially impairs use, market value, or safety of vehicle.
Period Covered:	One year or 15,000 miles, whichever is first.
Notice Requirement:	None specified.
"Reasonable" Repair Guidelines:	During period covered, either at least four repairs to same defect or at least 30 calendar days out of service for repairs, plus one final opportunity to cure by manufacturer. Creates presumption.
Affirmative Defenses:	Defect does not substantially impair use, market value, or safety of vehicle, or results from abuse, neglect, or unauthorized substantial modification or alteration by consumer. Statute of limitations: two years from end of period covered, extended while using informal settlement procedure.
Available Remedy:	Replacement or refund, at consumer's option.
Refund Details:	Full purchase price; incidental costs, including sales tax, registration fees, finance charges, options, and towing and rental costs. Deduction for use before first report of defect, and for all subsequent time when vehicle is not being repaired.
Other Remedies:	Mandatory reasonable attorney's fees to consumer. No limit on other consumer remedies. Violation is deceptive trade practice.
Arbitration:	If manufacturer maintains informal settlement procedure and notifies consumer at time of delivery, consumer must use either that procedure or state-run arbitration before entitled to replacement or refund.
Resale of Lemon:	Disclosure required.

South Carolina—S.C. Code § 56-28-10 et seq.

Vehicles Covered:	Private passenger motor vehicles designed, used, and maintained for the transportation of 10 or fewer persons, and sold and registered in state. Includes trucks weighing 7,000 pounds or less and demonstrators. Excludes motorcycles, motor-driven cycles, off-road vehicles, and living portion of motor homes.
Persons Covered:	Purchaser, lessor, and any person entitled to enforce warranty.
Use Covered:	Vehicle normally used for personal, family, or household purposes.
Defects Covered:	Defect that substantially impairs use, market value, or safety of vehicle, and does not result from accident, abuse, neglect, modification, or alteration.
Period Covered:	One year or 12,000 miles, whichever is first.
Notice Requirement:	Written notice to manufacturer, by registered, certified, or express mail, of need for repair and final opportunity to cure, but only if manufacturer clearly and prominently disclosed notice requirement at time of sale.
"Reasonable" Repair Guidelines:	During period covered, at least three repairs to same defect or at least 30 calendar days out of service for repairs. Creates presumption.
Affirmative Defenses:	Statute of limitations: three years from delivery.
Available Remedy:	Replacement or refund, at manufacturer's option.
Refund Details:	Full purchase price, including finance charges, sales taxes, license and registration fees, similar government charges, and other costs attributed to defect. Deduction for use before first report of defect.
Other Remedies:	Court may award costs, expenses, and attorney's fee to consumer.
Arbitration:	If manufacturer maintains informal settlement procedure, consumer must use either that procedure or state-run arbitration before entitled to replacement or refund.
Resale of Lemon:	Disclosure required; 12-month/12,000-mile warranty.

South Dakota—S.D. Codified Laws § 32-6D-1 et seq.

Vehicles Covered:	New, self-propelled vehicles intended primarily for use on public highways. Excludes motor homes and vehicles of 10,000 pounds or more.
Persons Covered:	Purchaser or any person entitled to enforce warranty.
Use Covered:	Vehicle used in substantial part for personal, family, or household purposes.
Defects Covered:	Defect that significantly impairs use, value, or safety of vehicle, and does not conform to warranty, and arises from ordinary use, and does not result from abuse, neglect, modification, alteration, or accident.
Period Covered:	Defect must first occur, and consumer must give notice of defect, within one year or 12,000 miles, whichever is first. Manufacturer must repair within two years or 24,000 miles, whichever is first.
Notice Requirement:	Written statement to manufacturer within one year or 12,000 miles, describing vehicle, defect, previous repair attempts, and those who attempted repair, and demanding correction. Manufacturer entitled to final repair attempt after notice.
"Reasonable" Repair Guidelines:	During two years or 24,000 miles, at least four repairs to same defect, plus final repair by manufacturer, or at least 30 calendar days out of service for repairs. Creates presumption.
Affirmative Defenses:	Defect does not significantly impair use, market value, or safety of vehicle, or results from abuse, neglect, or unauthorized modification or alteration. Statute of limitations: three years from delivery.
Available Remedy:	Replacement or refund, at consumer's option.
Refund Details:	Full contract price, including charges for dealer preparation and transportation, options, and non-refundable portions of service contracts; tax, license and registration fees, and other collateral charge; finance charges after first report of defect; incidental damages, including alternate transportation. Deduction for use before first report of defect.
Other Remedies:	Court may award reasonable attorney's fees to consumer.
Arbitration:	If manufacturer maintains informal settlement procedure, consumer must use before filing suit.
Resale of Lemon:	Disclosure required; title branded.

Tennessee—Tenn. Code § 55-24-201 et seq.

Vehicles Covered:	Self-propelled passenger motor vehicles, by which persons or property may be transported on highways. Excludes motorized bicycles, vehicles propelled by overhead electrical wires, motor homes, lawn mowers, garden tractors, recreational vehicles, off-road vehicles, and vehicles over 10,000 pounds.
Persons Covered:	Purchaser, lessee, transferee during express warranty term, or any persons entitled to enforce warranty. Excludes government entity and business entity with at least three vehicles.
Use Covered:	Vehicle not purchased for purposes of resale.
Defects Covered:	Defect that renders vehicle unreliable or unsafe for normal operation or reduces resale market value below average for comparable vehicles.
Period Covered:	Warranty term or one year, whichever is first.
Notice Requirement:	Written notice by certified mail directly to manufacturer of need for repair. Manufacturer entitled to final repair attempt if presumption exists at time of notice.
"Reasonable" Repair Guidelines:	At least three repairs to same defect or at least 30 calendar days out of service for repairs. Creates presumption.
Affirmative Defenses:	Defect does not render vehicle unreliable or unsafe for normal operation or reduce resale market value below average for comparable vehicles, or results from abuse, neglect, or unauthorized modifications or alterations by consumer. Statute of limitations: six months from end of period covered, extended while using informal settlement procedure.
Available Remedy:	Replacement or refund.
Refund Details:	Full purchase price, including all collateral charges such as sales tax, title, license and registration fees, other similar government charges, and other reasonable expenses. Deduction for use before first report of defect, and for all subsequent time when vehicle is not being repaired.
Other Remedies:	Court may award costs, expenses, and attorney's fees to consumer. No limit on other consumer remedies, but may not also obtain excess damages under lemon law.
Arbitration:	If manufacturer maintains informal settlement procedure and notifies consumer, consumer must use before entitled to replacement or refund.
Resale of Lemon:	No disclosure required.

Texas—Tex. Occ. Code § 2301.601 et seq.

Vehicles Covered:	Self-propelled vehicles with at least two wheels. Includes towable recreational vehicles, and engines, transmissions, and rear axles of vehicles over 16,000 pounds.
Persons Covered:	Retail purchaser entitled to enforce warranty, lessor or lessee, or transferee or assignee that is resident of state and is entitled to enforce warranty.
Use Covered:	Vehicle with primary purpose of transporting persons or property.
Defects Covered:	Defect that substantially impairs use or causes substantial loss in market value of vehicle; or life-threatening defect that creates substantial risk of fire or explosion, or that substantially impedes ability to control or operate vehicle for ordinary or intended use.
Period Covered:	Two years or 24,000 miles, whichever is first.
Notice Requirement:	Written notice mailed to manufacturer, and final opportunity to cure.
"Reasonable" Repair Guidelines:	At least four repairs to same defect, first two within one year or 12,000 miles, whichever is first, and next two within one year or 12,000 miles, whichever is first, of second repair; or at least two repairs to same serious safety defect, first one within one year or 12,000 miles, whichever is first, and second one within one year or 12,000 miles, whichever is first, of first repair; or at least 30 days out of service for repairs within period covered, with at least two repair attempts within one year or 12,000 miles, whichever is first. Creates presumption.
Affirmative Defenses:	Defect does not substantially impair use or market value of vehicle, or results from abuse, neglect, or unauthorized modification or alteration. Statute of limitations: six months from end of warranty term or period covered, whichever is first.
Available Remedy:	Replacement or refund.
Refund Details:	Full purchase price, plus reasonable incidental costs. Deduction for all use when vehicle is not being repaired.
Other Remedies:	No limit on other consumer remedies, but cannot recover lemon law remedies in action under Commercial Code.
Arbitration:	Consumer must use state-run arbitration before entitled to replacement or refund.
Resale of Lemon:	Disclosure required; 12-month/12,000-mile warranty.

Utah—Utah Code § 13-20-1 et seq.

Vehicles Covered:	New, self-propelled vehicles sold in state. Includes motor home chassis, and motorcycles designed for use on paved roads. Excludes off-road vehicles, living portion of motor homes, tractors, mobile homes, vehicles over 12,000 pounds, motorcycles designed for off-road use, electric bicycles, mopeds, motor scooters, and motor-driven cycles with engines under 150 cc or not over 5 horsepower.
Persons Covered:	Individual purchaser, lessee, or transferee.
Use Covered:	Vehicle intended primarily for use and operation on highways.
Defects Covered:	Defect that substantially impairs use, market value, or safety of vehicle.
Period Covered:	Warranty term or one year, whichever is first.
Notice Requirement:	None specified.
"Reasonable" Repair Guidelines:	Within period covered, at least four repairs to same defect or at least 30 business days out of service for repairs. Creates presumption.
Affirmative Defenses:	Defect does not substantially impair consumer's use of vehicle and does not substantially impair market value or safety of vehicle, or results from abuse, neglect, or unauthorized modifications or alterations by consumer.
Available Remedy:	Replacement or refund.
Refund Details:	Full purchase price, including all collateral charges. Deduction for use before first report of defect, and for all subsequent time when vehicle is not being repaired.
Other Remedies:	Court may award attorney's fees to prevailing party, whether consumer or manufacturer. No limit on other consumer remedies. Violation is unfair trade practice.
Arbitration:	If manufacturer maintains informal settlement procedure, consumer must use before entitled to replacement or refund. Consumer must submit claim to state before filing suit.
Resale of Lemon:	Disclosure required; title branded.

Vermont—9 Vt. Stat. § 4170 et seq.	
Vehicles Covered:	New passenger motor vehicles, still under manufacturer's express warranty, which are purchased, leased, or registered in state. Excludes tractors, snowmobiles, motorcycles, mopeds, living portion of motor homes, and vehicles over 12,000 pounds.
Persons Covered:	Purchaser, lessee for two or more years, transferee during express warranty term, or any person entitled to enforce warranty. Excludes government entities and businesses with at least three vehicles.
Use Covered:	Passenger vehicles.
Defects Covered:	Defect that substantially impairs use, market value, or safety of vehicle to consumer.
Period Covered:	Warranty term.
Notice Requirement:	Written notice to manufacturer, after presumption satisfied, of defect, election to proceed under lemon law, and election whether to proceed under manufacturer's settlement procedure or state arbitration. Manufacturer entitled to final repair attempt after notice.
"Reasonable" Repair Guidelines:	At least three repairs to same defect, at least one of which is within warranty term, or at least 30 calendar days out of service for repairs within warranty term. Creates presumption.
Affirmative Defenses:	Defect does not substantially impair use, market value, or safety of vehicle, or results from abuse, neglect, or unauthorized modifications or alterations by consumer.
Available Remedy:	Replacement or refund, at consumer's option.
Refund Details:	Full purchase price, including allowance for trade-in and down payment; finance and credit charges, registration fees, and similar incidental and consequential damages. Deduction for use before first repair attempt. State must also refund tax upon timely request.
Other Remedies:	Potential 10% penalty. Mandatory costs to consumer. Possible attorney's fees to prevailing party on unsuccessful appeal from arbitration. Lemon law remedy not available if consumer discontinued payments. Failure to comply is unfair or deceptive act or practice.
Arbitration:	Consumer must use either manufacturer's informal settlement procedure, if available, or state-run arbitration.
Resale of Lemon:	Disclosure required; title branded.

Virginia—Va. Code § 59.1-207.9 et seq.

Vehicles Covered:	Passenger cars, pickup or panel trucks, motorcycles, chassis of motor homes, and mopeds. Includes demonstrators and leased vehicles with warranties.
Persons Covered:	Purchaser, lessee, transferee during express warranty term, or any person entitled to enforce warranty.
Use Covered:	Vehicle used in substantial part for personal, family, or household purposes.
Defects Covered:	Defect that significantly impairs use, market value, or safety of vehicle by rendering vehicle unfit, unreliable, or unsafe for ordinary use or reasonable intended purposes, even if defect does not affect drivability.
Period Covered:	18 months, extended if defect not effectively repaired by end of period. Manufacturer entitled to final repair attempt after presumption satisfied.
Notice Requirement:	Written notice to manufacturer. Satisfied if manufacturer responds in writing to consumer's complaint, or if factory representative inspects vehicle or meets with consumer.
"Reasonable" Repair Guidelines:	Within period covered, at least three repairs for same defect, at least one repair for serious safety defect, or at least 30 calendar days out of service for repairs. Creates presumption of reasonable number of repair attempts and of significant impairment.
Affirmative Defenses:	Defect does not significantly impair use, market value, or safety of vehicle, or results from abuse, neglect, or unauthorized modification or alteration by consumer. Statute of limitations: 18 months from delivery or 12 months from final action of settlement procedure, whichever is later.
Available Remedy:	Replacement or refund. Consumer may choose refund.
Refund Details:	Full purchase price; all collateral charges, including sales tax, license and registration fees, finance charges and interest, transportation and preparation charges, and charges for options and service contracts; incidental damages. Deduction for use before first notice of defect.
Other Remedies:	Mandatory attorney's fees, expert fees, and costs to consumer. Mandatory attorney's fees, expert fees, and costs to manufacturer if action frivolous. Possible treble damages for failure to comply with arbitration award. No limit on other consumer remedies.
Arbitration:	If manufacturer maintains informal settlement procedure, consumer may use before proceeding under lemon law.
Resale of Lemon:	Disclosure required.

Virgin Islands—12A Virgin Islands Code § 180 et seq.

Vehicles Covered:	Self-propelled motor vehicles sold in territory, primarily designed for transportation of persons or property on roads or highways. Includes used vehicles with less than 50,000 miles, sold for $2,300 or more. Excludes vehicles run upon tracks, off-road vehicles, trucks over 10,000 pounds, and living portion of motor homes.
Persons Covered:	Purchaser, transferee during express warranty term, or any person entitled to enforce warranty.
Use Covered:	Vehicle used for personal, family, or household use.
Defects Covered:	Design or manufacturing defect that substantially impairs use, value, or safety of vehicle by rendering vehicle unreliable or unsafe for ordinary use or reasonable intended purposes, and that does not result from abuse, neglect, or unauthorized modification or alteration.
Period Covered:	Warranty term or one year, whichever is greater.
Notice Requirement:	Written notice to manufacturer, distributor, or dealer.
"Reasonable" Repair Guidelines:	New vehicles: at least four repairs for same defect, at least one of which is by manufacturer, or at least 40 business days out of service for repairs. Conclusively establishes reasonable number of repair attempts. Used vehicles: within warranty term, at least three repairs for same defect or at least 30 business days out of service for repairs. Creates presumption.
Affirmative Defenses:	Defect results from abuse, neglect, unauthorized modifications or alteration.
Available Remedy:	Replacement or reimbursement, at consumer's option.
Refund Details:	Full purchase price paid for vehicle, including allowance for trade-in; incidental costs, including interest. Deduction for all use by consumer up to time of replacement or refund.
Other Remedies:	Court may award costs, expenses, and attorney's fees to consumer. Court may award costs and reasonable attorney's fees to manufacturer for consumer's bad faith or frivolous claim. No limit on other consumer remedies.
Arbitration:	Consumer must submit dispute to Department of Consumer Affairs before filing suit.
Resale of Lemon:	Disclosure required.

Washington—Wash. Rev. Code § 19.118.005 et seq.

Vehicles Covered:	New, self-propelled vehicles originally purchased or leased in state and registered in state. Includes motorcycles, chassis of motor homes, demonstrators, and lease-purchases. Excludes vehicles purchased or leased by business as part of fleet of 10 or more vehicles, living portion of motor homes, and trucks of 19,000 pounds or more.
Persons Covered:	Any person entering into agreement or contract for transfer, lease, or purchase of new vehicle during period covered.
Use Covered:	Vehicles primarily designed for transportation of persons or property over public highways.
Defects Covered:	Defect that substantially impairs use, value, or safety of vehicle by rendering it unreliable or unsafe for ordinary use or diminishing its resale value below average resale value for comparable vehicles, and does not result from abuse, neglect, or unauthorized modification or alteration.
Period Covered:	Two years or 24,000 miles, whichever is first.
Notice Requirement:	Written request to manufacturer for replacement or repurchase. For motor homes, written notice to all manufacturers of need to repair defect after three repair attempts for same defect, or one repair attempt for serious safety defect, or 30 calendar days out of service for repairs; motor home manufacturers entitled to final repair attempt after notice.
"Reasonable" Repair Guidelines:	During period covered, at least two repairs for serious safety defect, at least one of which is within express warranty term; or at least four repairs for same defect, at least one of which is within express warranty term; or at least 30 calendar days (60 for motor homes) out of service for repairs, at least 15 of which are within express warranty term. Repair attempts deemed reasonable.
Affirmative Defenses:	Defect does not substantially impair use, value, or safety of vehicle, or results from abuse, neglect, or unauthorized modifications or alterations.
Available Remedy:	Replacement or repurchase, at consumer's option.
Refund Details:	Full purchase price, including allowance for trade-in but excluding rebate; collateral charges, including sales tax, unused license and registration fees, finance charges, insurance, transportation, preparation, and charges for service contracts and options; incidental costs, including expenses for repair, towing, and alternate transportation. Deduction for all use before manufacturer's acceptance of vehicle for repurchase or replacement.
Other Remedies:	Mandatory attorney's fees, costs, and additional damages of $25 per day to consumer prevailing in court after arbitration. Mandatory double and possible treble damages to prevailing party, whether consumer or manufacturer, for bad faith appeal of arbitration award. No limit on other consumer remedies. Violation is unfair or deceptive trade practice.
Arbitration:	Consumer must use either manufacturer's informal settlement procedure, if available, or state-run arbitration before filing suit.
Resale of Lemon:	Disclosure required; title branded.

West Virginia—W.Va. Code § 46A-6A-1 et seq.	
Vehicles Covered:	New passenger vehicles sold in state. Includes pickup trucks, vans, and chassis of motor homes.
Persons Covered:	Purchaser, transferee during express warranty term, or any person entitled to enforce warranty.
Use Covered:	Vehicle used primarily for personal, family, or household purposes.
Defects Covered:	Defect that substantially impairs use or market value of vehicle.
Period Covered:	One year or warranty term, whichever is first.
Notice Requirement:	Written notice to manufacturer, and opportunity to cure after notice. If no notice, no presumption of reasonable number of repair attempts.
"Reasonable" Repair Guidelines:	Within period covered, at least three repairs for same defect, or at least one repair for serious safety defect, or at least 30 calendar days out of service for repairs. Creates presumption if above notice given.
Affirmative Defenses:	Defect does not substantially impair use or market value of vehicle, or results from abuse, neglect, or unauthorized modifications or alterations. Statute of limitations: one year from end of warranty term, extended while using informal settlement procedure.
Available Remedy:	Replacement, or refund if consumer revokes acceptance and files suit.
Refund Details:	Purchase price, including sales tax, license and registration fees, and other reasonable expenses; cost of repairs; loss of use.
Other Remedies:	Court may award reasonable attorney's fees to consumer. No limit on other consumer remedies.
Arbitration:	If manufacturer maintains informal settlement procedure and notifies consumer, consumer must use before filing suit.
Resale of Lemon:	Disclosure required.

Wisconsin—Wis. Stat. § 218.0171

Vehicles Covered:	New motor-driven vehicles registered in state and purchased or leased in state. Includes demonstrators and executive vehicles. Excludes mopeds, semitrailers, and trailers designed for use with trucks or truck tractors.
Persons Covered:	Purchaser, lessee, transferee during express warranty term, or any person entitled to enforce warranty. Excludes purchaser at end of lease.
Use Covered:	Any.
Defects Covered:	Defect that substantially impairs use, value, or safety of vehicle and is covered under express warranty, and does not result from abuse, neglect, or unauthorized modification or alteration by consumer.
Period Covered:	Warranty term or one year, whichever is first.
Notice Requirement:	Report defect to manufacturer or any authorized dealer.
"Reasonable" Repair Guidelines:	Within period covered, at least four repairs for same defect or at least 30 calendar days out of service due to defects. Conclusively establishes reasonable number of repair attempts.
Affirmative Defenses:	None specified.
Available Remedy:	Replacement or refund, at consumer's option.
Refund Details:	Full purchase price, including sales tax and finance charges but excluding rebate; collateral costs, including repairs and alternate transportation. Excludes personal injuries. Deduction for use before first report of defect.
Other Remedies:	Mandatory double damages, costs, and reasonable attorney's fees to consumer. No limit on other consumer remedies.
Arbitration:	If manufacturer maintains informal settlement procedure, consumer must use before filing suit.
Resale of Lemon:	Disclosure required.

Wyoming—Wyo. Stat. § 40-17-101 et seq.	
Vehicles Covered:	Self-propelled motor vehicles under 10,000 pounds, sold or registered in state. Excludes vehicles moved solely by human power.
Persons Covered:	Purchaser, transferee during express warranty term, or any person entitled to enforce warranty.
Use Covered:	Any.
Defects Covered:	Defect that substantially impairs use and fair market value of vehicle to consumer.
Period Covered:	One year.
Notice Requirement:	Direct written notice to manufacturer, and reasonable opportunity to cure. If no notice and opportunity to cure, no presumption of reasonable number of repair attempts.
"Reasonable" Repair Guidelines:	Within period covered, at least three repairs for same defect or at least 30 business days out of service for repairs. Creates presumption if above notice given.
Affirmative Defenses:	Defect does not substantially impair use and fair market value of vehicle, or results from abuse, neglect, or unauthorized modification or alteration by consumer.
Available Remedy:	Replacement or refund.
Refund Details:	Full purchase price; collateral charges. Deduction for use before first report of defect, and for all subsequent time when vehicle is not being repaired.
Other Remedies:	Court may award reasonable attorney's fees to consumer. No limit on other consumer remedies.
Arbitration:	If manufacturer maintains informal settlement procedure, consumer must use before entitled to replacement or refund.
Resale of Lemon:	No disclosure required.

APPENDIX B

Bibliography

Books

Consumer Warranty Law—Lemon Law, Magnuson-Moss, U.C.C., Mobile Home and other Warranty Statutes
2nd Edition National Consumer Law Center (NCLC)

Don't Get Taken Every Time
The Insider's Guide to Buying or Leasing Your Next Car or Truck
by Remar Sutton
Penguin Books

The Car Book 2004
by Jack Gillis
America's Most Comprehensive Car Buying Guide
from the Center for Auto Safety

Lemon Law: A Manual for Consumers
by Norman F. Taylor and Merrell G. Vannier
Consumer Rights Center, 1991

Web Site References

www.alldata.com/tsb/

www.autosafety.org

www.campingworld.com

www.carconsumers.com/index.html

www.carfax.com

www.consumeraffairs.com

www.consumerlaw.org

www.consumerwatchdog.org

www.dca.ca.gov/acp/

www.dealer-magazine.com

www.dropbears.com/

www.findlaw.com

www.ftc.gov

www.goodsamclub.com

www.howstuffworks.com/engine2.htm

www.jdpower.com

www.mold-kill.com/isozonesafe.html

www.nhtsa.dot.gov/cars

www.rvjournal.com

www.rvusa.com

APPENDIX C

Glossary

Word	Definition
Arbitration	Arbitration is an informal process that consumers may use to resolve a warranty dispute outside of the court system by presenting it to a third party (i.e., the Dispute Settlement Board, Better Business Bureau, etc.) for a decision.
"As Is" Selling	A car that is sold "as is" is one which is sold with no warranty, such that the dealer or seller has absolutely no obligation to make any repairs, regardless of the vehicle's condition.
Collateral Charges	These are additional charges to a consumer that were incurred as a result of the acquisition of the vehicle. They usually include, but are not limited to, the following: charges for manufacturer-installed or agent-installed items, earned finance charges, use taxes, and title charges.
"Comparable" Vehicle	The manufacturer is required to replace the consumer's lemon vehicle with one that is either identical or reasonably equivalent.
Continuance	The postponement of the court proceedings in a case to a future day.
Court Order	An order issued by a court that requires a person to do or refrain from doing something.
Declaration	A statement made, not notarized, being offered as evidence.
Defendant	The party against whom a criminal or civil action is brought.
Due Bill	A brief written acknowledgment of a debt. For example, if at the time of delivery of your new car the dealership did not have the sound system you ordered, a "due bill" acknowledging the dealership's responsibility to provide the sound system of your choice is placed on the sales contract.
Expert	A person with special or superior skill or knowledge in a particular area.
Express Warranty	A written warranty, so labeled, issued by the manufacturer of a new motor vehicle. The express warranty provides certain promises concerning the vehicle's condition, fitness for use, and the manufacturer's obligations to repair, including any terms or conditions precedent to the enforcement of obligations under that warranty.
Lemon Car	The statutes define *lemon cars* and require that manufacturers (not dealers) remedy the defects. Most statutes define *lemons* as cars that continue to have a defect that substantially impairs the use, value, or safety of the car after a reasonable number of attempts to repair the car or after the car has been out of service for a particular number of days.

Letter of Notice to Manufacturer	A written statement which describes the motor vehicle, the defect, and all previous attempts to repair such defect(s), including identification of the person, firm, or corporation who made such attempts and time of such attempts. For example, you may want to include the following information: your name, address, and contact information; a description of the defect and all attempts to correct the defect; a description of the vehicle, including year, make, and model; the vehicle identification number, found on the registration; and a request that the manufacturer repair the defect.
Magnuson-Moss Act	The Magnuson-Moss law is a federal law giving consumers substantial rights in dealing with manufacturers of lemon cars.
Manufacturer-Sponsored Certified Arbitration	In order for a manufacturer-sponsored arbitration program to be certified in most states, it must meet the following requirements of the Federal Trade Commission (FTC) for mediation procedures: it must be free of charge; it must be non-binding to the consumer; its decisions must, in general, be given within 40 days after receipt of the buyer's complaint; and its decisions must be free from the influence of the manufacturer.
Mediation	Mediation does not require that you hire a lawyer and go to court. It can be preferable to arbitration because it is more flexible—allowing for more creative resolutions. Because both parties must provide consent to the resolution, it can be harder to get manufacturers to agree to—and to give—a refund or a replacement vehicle. However, most states do not offer mediation programs as part of their efforts to help consumers in lemon law disputes.
Odometer Rollback	If a more recent odometer reading is less than an older reading, then the odometer may have been "rolled back." This is an indicator of mileage fraud.
Ozonation	This can be an effective, yet less costly means of killing mold and mildew. Black toxic mold is a dangerous source of indoor air pollution. People who suffer from mold allergy are acutely aware of the discomfort caused by toxic mold exposure. Air conditioning systems in automobiles and motor homes may be susceptible to mold formation because the interior of the air conditioning system often becomes damp. Ozonation is one method of combatting this problem. It is not a permanent cure and may have to be done repeatedly.

Plaintiff	The party that institutes a law suit in a court.
Service Contracts (Extended Warranties)	Service contracts and extended warranties are functionally equivalent to each other. The consumer pays an additional amount to the seller or manufacturer for protections against product defects beyond those that are covered by the express and implied warranties. In some cases a service contract may actually be an express warranty.
Service Writer	Most large automobile dealerships have a person whose job it is to write up a repair order for each vehicle being brought in for repairs. This person is called a service writer.
Statute of Limitations	A statute setting a time limit on legal action in certain cases.
Subpoena	A writ requiring appearance in court to give testimony. To serve or summon with such a writ.
Substantially Impair	This means to significantly impair the use of the vehicle or a component of the vehicle, or to reduce its resale value below the average resale value for comparable motor vehicles. Certainly defects that cause the vehicle not to start, not to stop, or impair one's ability to operate the vehicle would be substantial impairments. However, significant paint defects or defects to key components, like the air conditioning system, might be considered substantial impairments as well. Whether a defect is a substantial impairment is a decision for the arbitrator, judge, or jury in a contested case.
SUV (Sport Utility Vehicle)	A four-wheel-drive vehicle with a roomy body, designed for off-road travel.
True Retainer	1. A client's authorization for a lawyer to act in a case. 2. A fee paid to a lawyer to obtain representation.
VIN (Vehicle Identification Number)	This 17-character number is unique to each vehicle. It identifies characteristics of the vehicle, including manufacturer, year, model, body, engine specifications, and serial number.
Warranty	A guarantee given on the performance of a product or the doing of a certain thing. For example, many consumer products come with warranties under which the manufacturer will repair or replace any product that fails during the warranty period, the commitment to repair or replace being the "warranty."

INDEX

Index

A

accessories, 140
air conditioning, 5
  asthma, 5–6
  mold problems, 5
arbitration
  another step in gauntlet, 153
  consumer and, 153
  dispute resolution settlement, 152
  do I have to go through arbitration, 11
  is rarely helpful, 95
  manufacturers love any kind of, 152
  manufacturers refer you to, 158
  mediation, 164
  to arbitrate or not to arbitrate, 151
as is sale, 130, 237
  buyer's guide warranty statement, 131
attempts to repair
  reasonable number, 88
  reasonable opportunity, 106
attorney
  fees. *See also* litigation
    consumers can recover, 160
    contingency fee agreement, 160
    shifting burden of, 162
  selecting an, 155

B

Band-Aid repairs, 119
Bar Association, 155
business use, 101
buybacks, different from other used cars, 169

C

CARFAX, 173
caveat emptor: let the buyer beware, xiii, 36
caveat venditor: let the seller beware, xiv
complexity
  and malfunctions, 52–59
  and quality, 53
  increased complexity leads to lemons, 53
computers
  check engine light on, car stalls, 4–8, 84–86
  diagnostic tools seldom find defects, 74
  dying brain, 58–59
  engine control computer (ECU), 55, 57–58
    garbage in, garbage out, 54
    Mercedes ditches glitches with electronics, 57
    no standardization in vehicle computers, 54
    software code, 54
    software design fault, 57

  vehicle sensors, 58
consumers can seek legal help, 60
Consumers for Auto Reliability and Safety, 169
corporate responsibility, 44
customer service, manufacturer
  agent, 9
  consumer hotline, 10
  customer satisfaction, 171
  customer service people are so nice, 91

D

damages
  civil penalty is additional penalty, 165–166
  consequential, 139
  incidental and consequential, 138–141
  insurance premiums, 138
  interest and finance charges, 138
  license and registration fees, 138
  loss of use, 138
  lost wages and profits at time of sale, 138
  personal injuries and property damage, 138
  rental car and travel expenses, 138
  repair and maintenance costs, 138
  sales tax, 138
  sales tax refund, 172
  towing and storage charges, 138
days out of service, thirty or more, 107
dealerships
  act on behalf of manufacturer, 109
  are big businesses, 61
  if you can't fix their car, 79
  must provide all repair orders, 109
  refusing to provide repair orders, 109
  visits to dealer, 5–11
  when dealership is in trouble, 75–77
    cutting pay, 76
    cutting people, 76
    slashing quality budgets, 76
    slashing training budgets, 77
    where they cut costs, 75
  why go to another, 92
dealer tricks, 84–91
  doesn't return calls, 88
  have I got a deal for you!, 90
  is intentionally rude, 90
  it's your fault, 86
  just bring it back, we'll fix it, 87
  little lady syndrome, 87
  no problem found, 87–88
  no repair order is written, 90
  offers to sell you new car, 90
  repair order alteration, 84
  slicing and dicing the defect, 85

that's the way it was designed to operate, 86
unable to duplicate malfunction, 88
we can't take your car now, 84
defective vehicles, number in America, 51–52
defects
  defined, 101
  latent, 35–36, 170
  substantial, 102–103
Deming, Dr. W. Edwards, 45–47
  and American manufacturers, 47
  quality chain reaction, 46
  quality revolution, 45–47
deposition, 164
DMV, California, action against Chrysler, 172
do not sign anything, 93
driver abuse, 144
due bill, definition, 4, 237

E

expert, 237
  automotive, 128, 163, 164
  he said, she said, 143–144
  when should I retain an expert, 156
express warranty is written warranty, 118, 237

F

flat-rate pay system
  after-warranty repair manuals, 74
  and potential recalls, 69
  dealerships love high-speed technicians, 73
  few repair shops guarantee minimum income, 71
  flagged hours, 71
  for technicians, 68–75
  how technicians are paid, 71–72
  intermittent problems, 75
  labor time manuals, 68
  part-swapping, 72–73
  recall example, 69
  recipe for disaster, 70
  vehicle diagnostics, 74–75
  work faster, not better, 73

G

gauntlet, 79–96. See also dealer tricks and stupid manu-
    facturer tricks
  manufacturer knows about problem, 80
  manufacturer toll-free numbers, 9, 91–92
  no problem found (NPF), 28, 79, 87–88
  oh, you again!, 28
  summary, 95–96
  technical specialist, 10, 92
  typical lemon gauntlet, 83
  we're too busy, 8, 84
  when it begins, 82
good deals, beware of, 159
  there are no good deals in gauntlet, 90–91, 93

H

how many people give up, 59

I

impaired
  safety, 105–106
  use, 103
  use does not mean no use, 103
  value, 104–105
implied warranty
  fitness for particular purpose, 122–123
  merchantability, 120
  not written down, 120
independent repair shops, 109–110
inexperienced mechanics, 57–58

J

J.D. Power and Associates, 47
Japanese automobiles at top, 47
Johnson, Samuel, 25
jury instructions, 163

L

lawsuit
  before lawsuit is filed, 156
  discovery as part of, 164
leased vehicles, 100
legal advice, seek as soon as possible, 154
lemon
  defined, 99, 237
  is your car legally a lemon, 99–115, 156
  not fit for intended use, 103
  vehicles that qualify, 100
lemon laundering, 167–173
  Automotive Consumer Notification Act, 40
  branding, 40, 173
  CA vs. Chrysler and manufacturer buybacks, 172
  flood-damaged cars, 169
  lemon law buyback decal, 40, 173
  notice of history of problems, 170
  permanent labeling, 173
  salvage vehicles, 169
  so-called goodwill buybacks, 170
  trade assists, 170, 171
  vehicle auction companies, 168
  what you can do about it, 173
lemon law
  California, xvi, 38
  cases, only 5-10% go to trial, 156
  consumers have no idea of, 60
  most state lemon laws apply to new products, 100
  presumption, 110
  requires a permanent cure, 119
  rights, 60
    consumers have no idea of, 60

don't sleep on your rights, 116
never waive, 92
lemon law, history of, 35–41
1250—St. Thomas Aquinas weighs in, 35
1603—England, caveat emptor, 36
1906—Uniform Sales Act, 37
1952—Uniform Commercial Code (U.C.C.), 37
1970—Song-Beverly Consumer Warranty Act, 38
1975—federal lemon law, 39
1982—Tanner Consumer Protection Act, 40
1991—Automotive Consumer Notification Act, 40
award of attorney fees, 38, 160–162
caveat emptor, 36
Chandelor v. Lopus, 36
early implied warranty of merchantability, 35
English common law, 37
latent defects, 35–36
lemon laundering, 40
nonconformity first defined, 40
lemon law, need for, 43
Dr. W. Edwards Deming, 45–47
every state has lemon laws, 43
lemon vehicle, cost of manufacturing, 50
level the playing field, 44
management ethics and greed, 48
quantity vs. quality, 44
quarterly financial report, 47
volume of defective consumer goods, 51–52
lemon law summary all fifty states, 175–229
litigation
before litigation, 154–159 See also prelitigation
don't take your vehicle back, 108
get vehicle repaired before returning it, 137
documents needed in court, 163
how long will it take, 163
if manufacturer loses, 160–162
manufacturer offers less than law allows, 158
manufacturer wants signed release of claims, 158
notifying manufacturer, 157, 238
offered car payments, 158
procedure, 162–164

M

Magnuson-Moss Act, 39, 99, 238
manufacturer(s), manufacturer's
breach of warranty, 117
improper maintenance, 146
modifications and alterations, 147
offer ten-year warranties, 117
responses, 157–159
manufacturer-dealership relationship, 61–77
goodwill gestures, 65
it's a business relationship, 61
secret warranties, 63–65
how do I learn about a secret warranty, 66–67
is disclosure of warranties required, 68
Technical Service Bulletins, 66
warranty adjustment policies, 65

warranty repair budgets, 62
manufacturer defenses, 143–149
improper maintenance, 146
modifications and alterations, 147
merchantability means fitness for ordinary use, 120
mileage allowance, 134
motor home lemon story, 15–23
American dream. See motor home lemon story
first visit: the defects, 17
four repair attempts, 19–23
jurisdictional issues, 16
motor home living area, 16
motor home slide-out, 19–22
multiple warranties, 16
pitfalls of, 20–21
repair facilities, 19
state sales tax, 15–16
tail wagging the dog phenomenon, 18
motor home warranties, 16, 118

N

National Highway Transportation Safety Association (NHTSA) can order recall, 63
never waive your rights, 92
new car lemon story, 3–13
dealership did not give repair order, 9
let the buyer beware, 3
new car purchase contract, 4
no more visits: they try arbitration, 11
six visits to dealer, 5–11
stalled in fast lane, 8
Nicklaus, Jack, 133
nonconformity same as defect, 101

O

oh, that's the way this model works, dear, 28
owner's manual, 91, 147

P

paper trail, 144, 156
proper paperwork is vital, 156
plaintiff, 110
prelitigation, 154, 163
inspection, 164
notifying manufacturer, 157
presumption, 110–115
burden of proof, 110–111
effect of lemon law presumption, 114
fee-shifting, 162
lemon period not a warranty period, 113

Q

quality
and the quarterly report, 47–48
product, 44
revolution in Japan, 45–47

R

Rand, Ayn, 15
recalls
  affect hundreds of thousands of vehicles, 65
  manufacturers do anything to avoid, 65
  whatever you do, hide the recall, 65
reconditioned or like new parts, 126
refund or replacement, 134, 160
  example of refund, 135
  example of replacement, 137
  remedy
    definition of, 133
    is your choice, 133
  repurchase your lemon, 167
release, don't sign, 93
repair attempts
  number of, xvii
  reasonable number, 88, 114–115, 163
repair order, 5
  keep all your repair orders, 107
  more on accurate repair orders, 84–86, 109
  never leave without, 144
repair visits
  all repair visits count, 107
  repeated repairs for same problem, 106–107
replacement, 136–137, 160
  or refund: choosing a remedy, 133–141
  with comparable vehicle, 167
return of defective vehicle, 137
revoke acceptance, 108
right way to handle defect, 43–44
Rumsfeld, Donald, 143

S

safety issues, examples, 105
safety restraint system warranty, 118
satisfaction guaranteed, Sears policy, 44
secret warranty
  check availability of goodwill assistance, 66
  is manufacturers' strategy, 65
  squeaky wheel gets the grease, 65, 68
  warranty adjustment policy, 65, 67
service contract(s), 123
  and warranties, 126
  buying, 128
  captive, 125
  coverage, 125–126
  defined, 123, 239
  does it duplicate warranty coverage, 129
  extended warranty, 123
  how are claims handled, 129
  how much does it cost, 129
  is optional repair coverage, 123
  no promise of quality, 126

owner responsibilities, 130
provide less coverage, 125
questions and answers, 129–130
what is covered and not covered, 129
who backs the service contract, 129
service labor time standards, 68
service writer, 5, 239
settlement conference, 164
shaken faith doctrine, 108
simple language vs. legalese, xviii
sport utility vehicle, 3, 239
statute of limitations, 148
  commercial code's statute, 149
  discovery rule, 148–149
  don't sleep on your rights, 116
  four-year statute, 149
stupid manufacturer tricks, 91–94
  bending over backwards to help you, 94
  don't get help, 94
  glad hand, 91–92
  just sign this release, Mr. and Mrs. Jones, 93–94
  try a different technician, 92
  we want to reward you for your patience, 92–93
substantial impairment, 102–106 *See also* defects, defined

T

taking delivery in another state, 15–16
Tanner Act, 40
teardown, 127–128
Technical Service Bulletins (TSBs), 66
technology, example of fundamental change in, 53
time, mileage, and days in shop, xviii
title branding, 171. *See also* lemon laundering
trade assists, 170–171
treating the symptoms, 59

U

Uniform Commercial Code (U.C.C.), 37–38
  applies primarily to commercial transactions, 38
unjust enrichment, 141
used car lemon story, 25–31
  are you sure you are using the right kind of gas?, 26
  engine knocking and pinging, 28–29
    dieseling, 29
  in-service date, 25
  six repair attempts, 26–30
  statute of limitations, 148
  summary, 31
  used car warranties, 26
  warranty runs out, 28
used vehicles, 100

V

vehicle(s)
    identification number (VIN), 173, 239
    in shop for more than 30 days, 31
    neglect, 147
    value not strictly monetary, 104
verbal offers, beware, 159
visits to dealer. *See* new car lemon story

W

warranty
    booklet, 91, 109
    bumper-to-bumper, 118
    express, 118
    full and limited, 118–119
    has time and mileage limit, 119
    how long does warranty last, 119
    implied, 120–121
    period is a discovery period, 119
    secret. *See* manufacturer-dealership relationship
    sheet metal and corrosion, 118
    state and federal emissions, 118
    what voids, 147
weight
    of RV poorly distributed, 18
    of truck may be significant, 101